WHAT PEOPLE ARE SAYING
INCREDIBLE BOOK

"I have known Phyllis for over 15 years and walked this journey hand in hand with her. Her commitment to excellence has always been number one. She is passionate about teaching others about entrepreneurship and vision. She is one of the most dedicated and hardworking people I know, and I am proud to call her a friend, a business partner, and family. I highly recommend this book."

Toni VanSchoyck
Network Marketing Professional
Independent Senior Executive Director, Monat Global

"Phyllis Marlene is an exemplary professional, entrepreneur, and community builder. She is a master networker who cares deeply about her clients and community and always aims to make meaningful connections and help up-level your business. She is always reliable, an amazing leader, and a loving, heart-centered human being with outstanding morals and ethics. I highly recommend this read."

Vanessa Raymond
International Speaker, Author,
and Confidence & Success Coach

"Phyllis genuinely takes an interest in everyone she meets, making it easy for her to become a master connector and networker. She's passionate about what she's doing and why. Phyllis will give you some of her secrets and best practices for business success and successfully transitioning from employee to entrepreneur. I highly recommend this book."

Carol Wachniak
CEO Doula Family Legacy Certification
Co-founder of the Fiji Foundation

"When I first met Phyllis in the UK at a women's business event in London, I was struck by her positive, dynamic approach to business. Some 5 years later, I saw the quantum leap that Phyllis had made in growing as an entrepreneur. She has demonstrated all the skills and attributes it takes to be successful. Her advice and guidance would be well-heeded, for Phyllis has phenomenal experience in a business world that has not been without its challenges.

"Driven and passionate, a great communicator, Phyllis deserves her success; she has worked for it. Never one to give up, she has proven by example the wisdom she shares within the pages of this book, which is a worthy read."

Caroline Purvey MA (Ed)
Founder TRE UK®
IAOTP, Top CEO of the Year in Alternative &
Holistic Health 2023

"It has been an incredible honor watching Phyllis go from wildly successful in the corporate world to wildly successful as an entrepreneur. She is doing incredible things for the world. Thank you, Phyllis, for showing the way to many women who would love to do what you have done."

Jean LaVallie
Founder and Owner, WESOS Network

"It's easy to relate to Phyllis. Her driving force as an entrepreneur is to support and fill the needs of everyone she connects with. After knowing her for over 15 years, she has always delivered on her promises and exceeded them. She strives to be the best and works on it every day. As we traveled to business conferences together, I've seen first-hand how she takes care of her team. I am honored to call her friend."

Judy Feldhausen
Holistic Health Practitioner, Speaker,
Best Selling Author

"Phyllis Marlene Benstein is a networking and communication expert providing new and existing business owners the tools to truly reach greatness. This book is highly recommended."

Robert Raymond
Achieve Systems CEO

BREAKING FREE FROM YOUR 9-TO-5

FROM DESK JOB TO DREAM BUSINESS IN 5 EASY STEPS

PHYLLIS MARLENE BENSTEIN

Foreword by Robert Raymond

ISBN: 979-8-89079-236-5 (paperback)
ISBN: 979-8-89079-228-0 (ebook)

Published by Jetlaunch Publishing (jetlaunch.net)

Dedication

This book is dedicated to my mom, Rhoda, my hero and role model for working hard, taking care of our family, and showing me that all things are possible. She's the spark that lit my fire to embrace who I was at my core, empower my inner change agent, embark on the journey out of corporate, evolve into the true and best version of myself, and enlighten others whose lights may be dimming.

I miss her. Mom was my biggest cheerleader. I am blessed, grateful, and thankful for the time we had together. She was my driving force for becoming an entrepreneur. Her spirit is shining down on me as I guide others to do the same.

TABLE OF CONTENTS

ENLIGHTEN

EXHIBITS

FOREWORD
BY ROBERT RAYMOND

When I was younger, I worked at a car wash, many restaurants, bars, and odd jobs. One day, I woke up and asked myself, "What the hell am I doing?" On this day, I shifted from employee to entrepreneur and business owner for the rest of my life. It was by far one of the most impactful and important days in my life.

It has had me on one incredible journey for the past 3 decades that has had its ups and downs but has been most rewarding. Anyone can make this move at any age. So don't allow Father Time or anyone to hold you back from making this happen. If you do not go for it, you might regret it for the rest of your life. Read that again, please. *If you do not go for it, you might regret it for the rest of your life.*

Today, because I made this decision, I am a 7-figure earner and multiple business owner; I wake up every day excited about the challenges ahead. If you want to make this happen, this book can provide important details to move forward. Some of the best advice I ever got was, "Don't reinvent the wheel because millions of people have done what you want to do. So, learn from them and implement what is right for you."

Networking, growing relationships, investing, and many other factors are only a small part of making the move from employee to entrepreneur and breaking free from your 9-to-5. You must create a strong plan and engage in different relationships that assist you in the journey. I would never transfer from employee to business owner without first writing a plan and then adding the necessary systems in my business that will lead to success. Many skip this step, so 8 of 10 people who open a business are out of business in a year or two. This book will help guide you with some outstanding tools to make it happen.

So many people today wish to shift from employee to entrepreneur to create freedom and financial independence in their lives. Having the right tools, knowledge, and resources will give you a huge advantage. I highly recommend you read this book and use the provided resources to help you succeed.

Congratulations!

Robert Raymond, #1 Ranked Business Coach, author of the *A5 Marketing Method*, owner of Achieve University, 8-time author, and one of the most sought-after business coaches today

NOTE TO READER

Are you *ready* to unleash your inner self, *empower* your evolution, step into your *greatness*, and **Break Free from Your 9-to-5**?

Look no further!

Close your eyes and imagine no longer having:

- Fear of failure
- Fear of the unknown
- Lack of discipline
- Lack of confidence
- Lack of faith
- Doubt
- To be stuck inside your comfort zone
- No accountability partner
- No strategy with measurable steps
- Lack of vision
- Lost hope
- Confusion about your why and/or purpose
- Trouble visualizing your compelling future
- Disbelief about what's possible

Imagine this: You spring out of bed, energetic and enthusiastic, ready and eager to do what you love and love what you do.

Now, compare that to your reality. Do you wake up lethargic and unenthusiastic, roll over, and hit the snooze button thinking, *Do I really have to go to work?*

Are you ready to unleash your inner self, empower your evolution, and step into your greatness? *Break Free from Your 9-to-5* is about finding personal freedom. It's time to take your first step today!

Do you know why most people don't have their dream job or live their dream life? It's because they either didn't have an exit strategy or didn't know how to start the transition.

Life is short! Are you living your life to the fullest? Are you ready to? Are you sick and tired of being sick and tired? Are you ready and willing to get comfortable being uncomfortable?

Congratulations on picking up this book! If you're reading this, you're likely contemplating a significant life change. Are YOU ready to *Break Free From Your 9-to-5* and start your journey from a desk job to creating your dream business?

You are taking the first step today!

WHAT'S HOLDING YOU BACK FROM LIVING YOUR DREAM LIFE?

UNCOVER GAPS AND CREATE A PLAN FOR THE LIFE YOU DESERVE

Tired of feeling stuck, unmotivated, or unfulfilled in your career?

After reading this book, your next step is to take the Take Control of Your Life Assessment.

Discover the obstacles in your path and map out a clear action plan to create a life of *freedom and fulfillment.*

Take the first step toward your dream life now:
breakingfreefromyour9to5.com/assessment

EMBRACE

1
MY PROFESSIONAL JOURNEY AND STORY

I had very humble beginnings.

My mom, Rhoda, is my hero and biggest influence. With her dedication to family combined with her work ethic, she was a great role model.

Mom was a registered nurse who worked the night shift so she could be home to get me off to school. She slept while

I was at school so we could have a normal afternoon and evening. Then, she went to work while I was sleeping. She was confident, educated, and funny. She loved the finer things in life, and our home was always filled with music. She taught me to be the best and unique version of me. She always said that anyone can be ordinary and like everyone else, but beauty comes from being different and standing out.

I've carried that saying with me my whole adult life. Some of the other things she taught me were that being unique is special, to be myself, to be genuine, and to see the good in everyone. She enrolled me in piano and dance lessons at age 5. We also frequented the off-Broadway musicals in Philadelphia.

My dad, Jack, was a mathematician and computer programmer. He taught me to find my passion, no matter what I decided to do in life. Dad taught me to love math at an early age. Years later, he strongly suggested I go into a math-related field. Starting in kindergarten, I learned math in the car with Dad while running errands. Where most kids would be singing songs with their parents, Dad and I were going over math tables. It paid off many years later, as I took a pre-college math SAT in 8th grade to see how advanced I was. I got the state's first 800.

When I got to high school, I was placed in Advanced Algebra. I even became president of the school's math club. After school, we practiced math problems. Then, we competed at different schools with timed tests.

In addition to instilling in me to be the best at what I did, my dad also emphasized always being at the top of my game. Unsurprisingly, I became a math whiz with great training from my dad. I went to engineering school since he wouldn't pay for me to go to Carnegie Mellon or NYU Greenwich Village to pursue my other dream of being an actress and musician.

Although I later found out my roots and heart were in the fashion and beauty industry, I graduated with a Bachelor of Science in Electrical Engineering. I began a 25-year career in a male-dominated, fast-paced, demanding environment. I was a high-frequency RF design engineer. I loved my job and the intellectual stimulation but needed some new creative and positively inspiring challenges.

I went to work in the dark; I came home in the dark. I traveled extensively and sacrificed time with my precious children to climb the corporate ladder. I had little work-life balance. However, I loved that JOB for many years. (If you haven't heard, JOB stands for "journey of the broke.") I sacrificed precious time away from my 4 beautiful children: Rachel, Shannon, Michael, and Mack.

For 25 years, I worked an average of 50 or more hours a week as an electrical engineer. During that entire time, I worked with only a few women.

Near the end of my career—which I voluntarily left and self-retired from at the ripe young age of 48—I watched many others go to work in the dark, come home in the dark, work long hours, travel, and be a servant to someone else's company with many sacrifices. It was running on a circular hamster wheel with no exit strategy. My whole career was about rising above negativity and egotism, proving myself, and achieving balance while helping other women do the same.

Thirteen years into my career, I had 4 beautiful kids, a negative husband, and an intense job. Through this journey, I discovered I loved networking and building authentic relationships with others. By listening and connecting the dots of what we did through conversations, I became known as a master connector.

With the suggestion of one of my male mentors, an executive VP who had a daughter in engineering with similar struggles, I started a women's networking group at my company with social, educational, and philanthropic aspects. Over the years, it became a benchmark for all the other divisions nationwide to implement.

Then, coincidentally, many years later, a girlfriend and I decided one day that we needed to meet other men and women outside of our company as well as in our community. We attended a local networking event. Little did I know that one event would change the trajectory of my life forever.

We attended, and I joined, a local Women In Business group where I could get back to talking to people. At the time, I was spending many hours in a laboratory, which did not give me much opportunity to network. Always inspired by successful women, this networking atmosphere breathed new life into me. I learned a lot, made great friends, and was invited to their annual awards night.

They had a vendor opportunity at the awards event. My mom, a powerful, successful Tupperware lady, got a table to promote her business. Mom had gently tried to get me to look closer at what she was doing with Tupperware for years. Although I had grown up in that environment, as she retired from nursing to dive into Tupperware, I wasn't interested. Why would I be? I was a degreed electrical engineer with 4 little kids at home; I had an over full-time career and an unhappy marriage.

Through what I would call a domino chain of events, I was introduced again to the wonderful world of network marketing. My mom pushed me to continue the conversation. My new friend, Paula, who was a leader with a well-known skincare company, got me at, "If you knew you couldn't fail at this, what is the one thing you most desire that would make you want to give this a try?" and "How many hours a week could you spare to work on it?"

My mom answered first for me: to stay at home with my young kids with an executive income. I answered that I had about 2 hours a week—max!

Paula then asked, "If I showed you how to start your business with 2 hours a week and build to staying home, would you do it?"

I signed up on the spot because I had the gut feeling for a while that I was meant for more: I was subconsciously looking for a way out of corporate jail. I took out a loan with my credit union to purchase my initial inventory. I fell in love with the vehicle to serve others while making others look and feel good.

My 2 hours turned into 4, then 8, then more, as I made time for my biggest priority: my kids. I learned to compartmentalize my feelings and my work to start to achieve work-life balance.

I also got the courage to divorce my first husband. I was able to pay off over $40,000 in divorce proceeding debt with my little network marketing side hustle. I'm not suggesting this be your path, but it worked amazingly for me.

Thank goodness for all the support surrounding me while I built my confidence. At the same time, others were showing me the potential of a different path to mental, financial, and personal freedom.

My first business as an entrepreneur was a chance for me to be in a nurturing environment of other women. This was step one of my journey to overcoming a trapped existence of my true self at my core. I had a new outlook on life, a new wardrobe and make-up, and the awakening sleeping giant within me to be all I could be. This allowed me to enrich the lives of others and to pay it forward to help other women step out of mediocrity and be all they could be. I was finally working toward work-life balance.

Fast forward 10 years: I built an amazing team, earned a free car, and became a director. Yet, I still had that engineering ball-and-chain job that held me from unleashing my true inner self, dreams, and passions. However, God had a different plan for me.

Fast-forward another 3.5 years: I had reinvented my life and myself. I married my best friend, soul mate, and confidant, Harry Benstein. I had become very successful in my next company. What a freeing experience! Never in my wildest dreams had I imagined this would be my path. Now, I wake up excited, renewed, grateful, and passionate every day to start the day doing what I love and loving what I do. Is this your dream, too? My passion is to help others like you be all they can be, follow their hearts and dreams, and rise above the everyday ordinary.

I was on a new career path by working for myself. The new me had transformed mentally on the inside; I had a whole new vibe and look on the outside. I also had a fierce determination to go out, show up, and make an impact on those around me. Do you desire to make a bigger impact? I had some work to do to let the world know I had changed directions, with a new mission, vision, and purpose to share so others could emerge from similar situations.

You know the saying: You are most like the 5 people you hang around with. It was time for a new crowd. I joined new organizations for personal and professional development. I joined both national and international networking organizations to attend, speak at, sometimes sponsor, and, most importantly, learn from. After a very short time, I began to lead groups and chapters to share my expertise while strengthening my new brand. I spoke internationally in my field of natural beauty and wellness products. I have also been published in many magazines and collaborative international bestselling books.

What drove me to do this major shift? How did I do it? Are *you* ready to embark on your journey?

I loved my JOB and the technical, geeky aspects for a very long time. However, my values and passions didn't align with my life dreams and goals after a while. I'm one to regularly evaluate what I'm doing and where I'm going. I looked up to the successful women and men in my field. Some loved it, and some didn't.

I made it to a particular level of leadership in corporate, only to find that the more you work and the better you do, the more responsibility you get. There was also more back-stabbing, dishonesty, office politics, long hours, travel, and increasing time away from family and friends, who were the passions inside me that made my heart sing. I then evaluated what success meant to me, where I wanted to be in 5 years, and what I wanted to accomplish. I turned to my mentors and role models and took some self-discovery and self-development workshops to discover and define my next steps and desired path and outcome.

Some people can wing it through life. However, those with written goals and a roadmap have more success and end up where they intend; they don't just happen upon it. Courage, faith, and a strong belief in myself, my abilities, and my dreams inspired me to keep moving forward and not look back.

Insanity, to me, is doing the same things repeatedly to get by and not ahead. I have an inborn desire to be the best version of myself, rise above the sea of mediocrity, and make a huge difference to my family first, then work outward to the others in my life with whom I come in contact.

I took some time to discover the beauty in the world around me and the rich relationships I could enhance once I embarked on the trip out of corporate. I learned many years ago that women, especially, have lower self-esteem and con-fidence. This is a by-product of the daily rat race, negative environment, and trying to please everyone at the expense of themselves. Once anyone develops confidence and self-esteem, they can do anything they desire and start on their path of being extraordinary and unstoppable!

Another part of my journey was changing the people I associated with and the groups I belonged to. I chose a different crowd of people who were enthusiastic, energetic, and passionate about what they did or stood for. I needed to associate with this type of crowd. Remember, you are most like the 5 people you hang around most. Being in the presence of others vibrating at a higher level made me do the same.

After participating in high-level networking groups through interactions and contacts, I became a master networker, connector, and collaborator. I enjoy looking for and finding the synergies between people and their businesses and passions in life.

I then decided to do a personal strengths and tools analysis and attended many personal and business development courses and workshops. Knowledge is power. I began to learn so much more than my engineering life had exposed me to. There was amazing content, resources, and a whole new channel of supercharged entrepreneurs to meet and engage with. I am very grateful for the connections, opportunities, and visibility these various groups provided.

Through networking and masterminding, I have teamed up with other visionaries. I continue collaborating with others on programs and projects to enrich others' lives and businesses.

NETWORK MARKETING: MY FIRST BUSINESS AND BEYOND

I joined my first beauty, health, and wellness network marketing company 25 years ago. This began the most incredible journey of a lifetime for not only me but also for my husband and kids.

I lead, train, and inspire large teams for a different company. My teams include hair and beauty professionals, stay-at-home moms, corporate employees and executives, nurses, teachers, lawyers, influencers, business leaders, and a blend of other professionals. Notice the vast array of industries I have been able to cross into because of my passion for helping people be more than they have ever been in business.

I show men and women how to run successful businesses, get paid what they are worth, and design the life of their dreams on their terms. They build their businesses by selling beauty, health, or wellness products, educating others, and helping others create and start lucrative businesses.

I seriously and intentionally help others awaken their sleeping giants as someone helped me awaken mine. When you awaken these giants, you'll discover that you truly are meant for more. You'll then be able to start a new path, irrespective of your age, like I did. Many of the people I work with quickly see that their ages are not a factor in their quest for success in business and life.

Age, indeed, is just a number. It should not be considered a limitation to achieving one's goals and aspirations. It is never too late to realize that there is something more you were meant to do. There is no better time than the present to embark on this journey toward personal growth, new beginnings, or life or career changes.

It is easy to find ourselves stuck in a certain mentality or routine, believing we've missed our chances or that it is too late to pursue our passions. However, this belief couldn't be further from the truth. Life is full of surprises and opportunities. Realizing you are destined for more is the beginning of a new, exciting chapter in your life.

Over time, I have also added to my repertoire realizing the importance of multiple income streams. I have acquired a brand of networking chapters worldwide called Connect and Collaborate. This event system in a box is associated with Achieve Business Systems, where I am the networking and community director, Alpha leader, and board member. This business allows me to use my master skills in connection, networking, and building million-dollar relationships through collaboration. In addition, I also provide even more resources for entrepreneurs to grow and scale their businesses and have greater visibility. What can you add to what you are currently doing to grow and scale your business and have greater visibility?

I can strongly attest to the fact that my success in business has been the result of several key elements:

- Awareness
- Learning key skills in verbal and nonverbal communication
- Having an image that represents my brand and me
- Networking

ARE YOU READY TO TAKE THE FIRST STEP TODAY? As you read this book, I will help you through this process.

2

RECOGNIZING THE LITTLE PUSHES AND SIGNS

Mental Signs of Change

There were mental signs screaming inside my head that grew louder and louder as time went on. Do you also have these voices in your head? They were not-so-subtle signs leading me to the final breaking point and, ah, the glass ceiling—being overlooked for promotions I was overqualified for, especially in engineering.

Oh, you're unhappy. Go back to school, get a new degree, and switch companies.

Since you are reading this book, are you ready, like I was, to figure out what you've become an expert at, combine that with your core passions and beliefs, and monetize it?

Are you also:

- Sitting at work, thinking, *This JOB is no longer in alignment with my core values.*
- Then thinking, *I didn't work my butt off for others to take credit for my work!*
- And then, *I never imagined I'd work for men less intelligent than me or that women in tech still don't make as much as men.*
- Or better yet, being promoted because the company had a minority- or women-owned business quota to meet to get their next contract. Geez!

For me, this negativity was overwhelming at times. To see the unhappy faces of employees dragging themselves to work every day because they didn't explore their options or had planned exit strategies.

The physical signs were telling me I needed to make a change. The signs included headaches, heart palpitations, backaches, IBS, anxiety, and a whole lot of stress. On the family side, I was craving work-life balance.

What physical and emotional signs are YOU having?

_____

_____

God works in mysterious ways.

I've always been very in tune with my body. One day, I felt a moving lump in my left abdomen. It ended up being a growing, fluid-filled ovarian cyst that grew to about the size of an orange. My gynecologist did some testing. There was a grainy portion that could've possibly been cancer. I was scheduled for and had a full hysterectomy with a vertical incision that ran between my belly button and my pelvic bone. By the grace of God, there was no cancer.

I then had to take 6 weeks off from work. However, as a result of being so exhausted, the 6 weeks turned into 8 weeks. During those 8 weeks, in the beginning, I worked my business from a recliner or a lawn chair for a few hours a day. I worked more near the end of the 8 weeks. This downtime finally gave me the time to reflect and re-evaluate my career, my vision, my time with my family, and the lifestyle I wanted for myself and my family.

At the end of those 8 weeks, I had a burning desire to get out of corporate. It felt so good to spend a few hours, even with low energy, sitting outside in the warmth of the sun, listening to the birds, and smelling the beautiful flowers all around me. I realized at this point how fragile life was. I also realized that life could turn in a minute, and I needed to start following my heart.

I was a mere 48 years old when I realized that there is more greatness inside of me to serve more people on a grand or grander scale—and it wasn't happening with me sitting at my desk working for someone else in a cesspool of negative, backstabbing, and unmotivated engineers.

In my first year in engineering, I worked about 60 hours a week because I got hired for a project that was behind schedule. This was the *first sign:* Is this the life I wanted?

Then, I got married 7 months into my first job. The hours were manageable until I started to have my 4 amazing children. I worked 10 minutes from home and was the parent on call for any kid emergency, of which there were many. I cherished my time with my kids, but my nanny raised my kids for a while as I had long hours. Then, travel was added. I got into the habit of bringing work home with me.

Somewhere in this segment was easily the *second sign*: Did I realize that little by little, my work-life balance had degraded so much? No, not yet.

Have you heard the phrase, "You can't see the whole picture if you're in the frame"? Well, I was in the frame. This saying refers to the idea that our perspective can be limited or biased when we are too close to something or too emotionally invested in a situation. It suggests that we must step back and gain some distance to see the bigger picture and gain a more objective view.

This saying is often used to encourage people to reflect on their situation and assess it objectively rather than being overwhelmed by their emotions or personal biases. It can be particularly helpful when making important decisions or facing challenging circumstances. I'm grateful I stepped out of the frame during my medical leave.

Three other things happened that became the tipping point for me in deciding to leave the corporate setting, take my toolbox, which had grown extensively, and start my own business.

Situation 1: I grew up being a Girl Scout. My parents were den leaders for my brother's Boy Scout troop. I couldn't wait to volunteer to be a Daisy leader for my 2 daughters when they got to kindergarten. We took the Daisy troop on a cabin camping trip one snowy weekend. At night, as the girls played together after our organized activities, the moms had a chance to hang out. *It was mortifying for me.* I couldn't relate to their stay-at-home trials and tribulations; they couldn't relate to my engineering world. That trip sparked a huge fire in me, and I needed to make some changes. I had wanted those kids and to be a mom, yet I sacrificed many years of time with my kids because of work and travel. This was about halfway through my career, about 12 years into it.

Situation 2: After my divorce, my position at work was as a program manager. The position required overtime and travel. I was in a situation that started a decade of being a single mom; I needed some allowances in my schedule and job.

Shortly after I explained this to my management, I got called into a meeting with the vice president of our division, David N, and the manager in charge of the program managers at my site, Michael P. The vice president said I needed to choose between my job and my kids because I couldn't stay in my current position. Which would it be? I answered right away, "My kids."

Then, the manager said, "We will find you another job in the company." I said, "No, I'll find my own," and I did. Looking back, I could've sued them. But I really needed my job because I was a single mom of 4 kids with an ex-husband trying to push me into bankruptcy, even though we were doing a dual-parenting arrangement. This was a huge sign that this JOB was going and growing against my core values.

The next situation, though, was the one that broke the camel's back, the ultimate tipping point for me.

Situation 3: In my 25-year career, I never had a female boss, and I had only one woman ever work directly for me. I'm super smart: a math whiz and analytical. One of my core skills is my ability to take extremely complex problems and situations and break them down into easy-to-understand terms for my peers and customers.

My very last position before I quit working was on parts obsolescence. I worked for a government defense contractor and was one of the experts in finding aircraft replacement parts or development proposals for redesigns if parts couldn't be obtained. My last set of bosses was ruthless. My department boss obviously had a stay-at-home wife. He never had to deal with employees with mom issues. On top of that, he never stayed current, which, in my mind, is key to a successful engineering career.

I had another boss who oversaw managing the overall obsolescence projects. He assigned me lots of problems, took credit for my work, and presented it in meetings I was not invited to. Guess what happened to him? After I quit, he eventually lost his position. He had a supervisor under him, and I was eventually assigned to him. I brought so much money and work into the department that my supervisor was able to hire 2 emerging engineers on a fast-track rotation. So, what happened that caused me to quit?

It seems like yesterday, but I have since realized that I owe these incredibly incompetent, unprofessional men a *thank you*. I would not be the successful entrepreneur I am today if I hadn't had that push out of my career.

So here goes: One day, I was called to my supervisor's office for my annual review. Typically, raises were 3 to 5 percent, depending on the budget and economy. I had done great but was told I was getting a 0 percent raise for the coming year due to my 0 percent contribution to the organization. In reality, I knew I was a threat to these guys: a young, really smart, professional, current woman engineer. At first, I was hurt. I went back to my office to have a very short pity party. Then, I got angry—very angry. I turned that anger into fuel to decide to look for a path out and to develop my exit strategy.

I stayed in Corporate America for another year. I was well-known and respected by industry leaders and those in the niche technical groups I participated in.

A few months later, my company offered a voluntary layoff. After consulting with my husband, I applied and was accepted. No one should have to endure the negativity and disrespect I endured over the many years of my career. During some discussions before I left, I also discovered that in 2011, I still wasn't paid the same as my male counterparts.

I've read other "Woe is me" books about poor victims trapped in corporate hell. We all know the drill—how unfairly you've been treated. What are *you* going to do about it?

We are in control of our destiny. You are the captain of your ship. Your life is a reflection of *your* decisions.

ARE YOU SICK AND TIRED OF BEING SICK AND TIRED?

Are you truly happy with your ordinary life of mediocrity?

Are you truly happy building someone else's company?

Corporations use people to build their businesses. However, by being an entrepreneur, you can grow your business by building up people as you serve them with your products and services.

Do you have a feeling deep in your gut that you were meant for more or that you have untapped gifts to share?

Have you ever woken up in the morning and felt drained, like you were already behind on the day before it even began? Do you dread going to work, knowing it's just another day of grinding away at someone else's goals and dreams while yours go unfulfilled?

Are you sick and tired of being sick and tired?

Well, my friend, you're not alone. Millions of people all around the world are living the same kind of mediocre, unfulfilling lives you are. They're building someone else's company, working long hours to make someone rich, and sacrificing their dreams and aspirations.

However, what if I told you there was another way? What if I told you that you don't have to settle for a life of mediocrity and that you can be your own boss, make your own rules, and build the life you truly want?

As an entrepreneur, you can take control of your destiny. You can start your own business, create your own products or services, and serve your customers in a way that brings you joy and fulfillment. You can build people up as you grow your business, creating a culture of empowerment and success that benefits everyone involved.

It all starts with you. You have to believe in yourself and your abilities. You have to be willing to take a risk and chase your dreams. You have to be willing to put in the work, learn from your mistakes, and persevere in the face of challenges and setbacks.

If you're truly *sick and tired of being sick and tired,* you owe it to yourself to make a change. You owe it to yourself to take that first step toward living the life you truly want.

What are you waiting for? The time to start is *now*.

ARE YOU BURNT OUT?

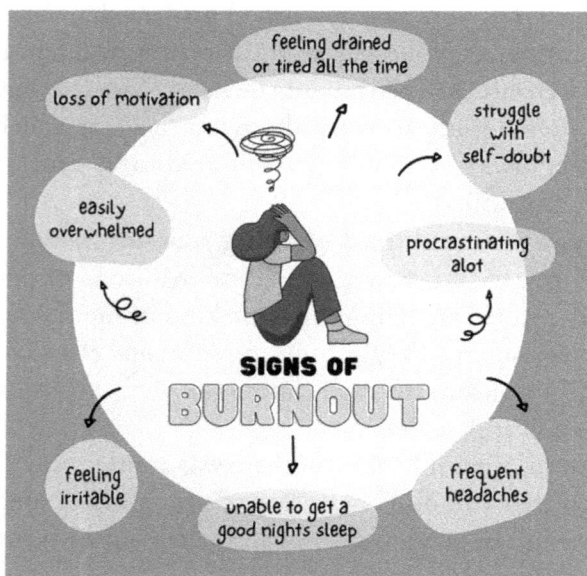

SIGNS OF BURNOUT IN A CORPORATE JOB

It's easy to fall into the trap of overworking yourself in a corporate job without realizing its negative effects on your mental and physical health. Burnout is common among workers in high-pressure jobs such as finance, law, and tech. Burnout often causes a decline in work performance and overall dissatisfaction.

Here are some warning signs that you may be experiencing burnout in your corporate job:

1) Chronic exhaustion
2) Lack of motivation and productivity
3) Increased irritability and impatience
4) Detachment from work and colleagues
5) Diminished overall satisfaction in life

If you find yourself experiencing these symptoms or know someone who is, continue reading to find out what you can do to combat burnout in your corporate job.

WHY BURNOUT OCCURS IN CORPORATE JOBS

Burnout results from chronic stress and overworking yourself without taking the necessary breaks to recharge. Corporate jobs demand a high level of performance. That high level of performance often leads to overworking and neglecting self-care. The pressure to meet deadlines, complete projects, and exceed expectations in the workplace can also lead to a heightened sense of anxiety and urgency.

Moreover, many corporate cultures promote always being "on" and working around the clock. This also leads to burnout. Employees who fail to meet the corporate culture's demands or the job's expectations may be subjected to scrutiny, criticism, or even termination, causing heightened work-related stress.

STRATEGIES FOR COPING WITH BURNOUT IN A CORPORATE JOB

If you are experiencing burnout in your corporate job, don't panic. There are several strategies you can implement to mitigate the negative effects of chronic stress and avoid burnout:

1. **Prioritize Self-Care:** Take time to do the things you enjoy and unwind after work. Indulge yourself with relaxation activities like yoga, reading, or a warm bath.
2. **Set Boundaries:** Know your limits and stick to realistic goals. Don't take on too much work at once. Learn to say *no* to excess responsibilities instead of over-committing yourself.
3. **Seek Support:** Talk to someone you trust about your feelings of burnout, an understanding colleague, a friend, or a licensed professional.
4. **Take Time Off:** Take a short break from work to rest and recharge. Use your vacation days to take a trip or relax at home for a few days.

OVERCOMING FAILURE AND OBSTACLES: TURNING SETBACKS INTO GROWTH AND LEARNING OPPORTUNITIES

As an entrepreneur, you will undoubtedly face failure and obstacles on your journey. However, the key to success is not avoiding these challenges but learning how to overcome them and turn them into growth opportunities.

1. **Reframe Failure as Feedback**: When entrepreneurs experience failure, they often feel discouraged and defeated. However, it's important to reframe failure as feedback. Failure can teach you valuable lessons and help you course-correct your strategy. Instead of seeing failure as a personal reflection of your abilities, view it as an opportunity to gather feedback and improve.
2. **Learn from Others**: Entrepreneurship can be lonely, but you don't have to face challenges alone. Seek out mentors, join entrepreneur groups, and network with like-minded individuals. Learning from others who have faced similar challenges can help you gain perspective, identify blind spots, and find new solutions.
3. **Embrace a Growth Mindset**: Having a growth mindset means seeing challenges as opportunities to grow and learn. Instead of believing that your intelligence and abilities are fixed, believe you can improve through hard work and dedication. Embracing a growth mindset can help you stay motivated and persistent, even in adversity.
4. **Break Challenges Down into Smaller Steps:** Large, complex obstacles can seem overwhelming and impossible to overcome. However, breaking them down into smaller steps can make them more manageable. Identify the specific actions you need to take to address the challenge and tackle them one at a time. This can help you build momentum and find success in small victories.
5. **Stay Committed:** Entrepreneurship is not for the faint of heart. It takes grit, determination, and a long-term commitment to succeed. Stay focused on your vision and goals, even when faced with setbacks and obstacles. Remember that failure is not the end but a stepping stone on your journey to success.

By reframing failure, learning from others, embracing a growth mindset, breaking challenges down into smaller steps, and staying committed, you can overcome failure and obstacles and turn them into opportunities for growth and learning.

SIGNS TELLING YOU IT'S TIME TO EXIT THE CORPORATE RAT RACE

Leaving your job is a big decision. It can feel overwhelming and scary to know that stepping away from your current position could lead to an uncertain future. However, sometimes, it's the right thing to do. In those cases, it's important to be aware of the signs and pushes telling you to leave your job.

One of the most common signs that it's time to leave your job is when you're no longer being challenged. If you're bored with the tasks you're given or find you're no longer learning any new skills, it might be a good time to consider a new job. You should feel challenged and engaged in the work you do. If that's no longer the case, it's probably time to move on.

Another sign it might be time to leave your job is if you feel unmotivated. If you're not enjoying your job or don't feel excited about going to work, it's probably time to find something new. You shouldn't have to dread going to work every day; you should feel motivated and inspired by your work.

It's also important to consider other pushes that might be telling you to leave your job, such as physical symptoms and stress. Stress can manifest itself in physical symptoms such as tense muscles and headaches. If this is the case for you, it's likely time to start looking for a new job. Stress can also take a toll on your mental health, leading to depression and anxiety. If this is the case, it's a sign that it might be time to leave.

Finally, it's important to consider your long-term goals. It may be time to leave if you're no longer growing or learning in your current job or don't feel like you're moving closer to your goals. Consider your ideal job and whether your current position is helping you get there.

Leaving a job can feel intimidating and scary. However, by being aware of the signs and pushes telling you to move on, you can be confident that leaving your job is the right decision.

WHY OPEN YOUR OWN BUSINESS?

Freedom	Financial independence	To be your own boss
Creativity	Travel	Rewards
Opportunity	Leadership	Become an influencer
Make a bigger impact	Pursue your passion	Personal growth
Flexibility	Professional growth	Autonomy
Creating a legacy	Solving a problem	Control
Opportunity	Challenge	Lifestyle change

3

OVERCOMING FEAR AND BUILDING CONFIDENCE

The journey to *Break Free From Your 9-to-5* is filled with challenges, and fear is one of the most significant obstacles. Fear of failure, fear of the unknown, and fear of stepping out of a comfortable routine can all be paralyzing.

However, any aspiring entrepreneur must overcome these fears while building confidence. Just as focus shapes your reality, your ability to confront and conquer fear will determine the trajectory of your entrepreneurial journey.

THE POWER OF FEAR AND CONFIDENCE

Fear, in many ways, is a natural response to the uncertainty that comes with new ventures. It is the mind's way of protecting you from potential dangers. However, when fear dominates your thoughts, it can prevent you from taking the risks often required in entrepreneurship. The key is not to eliminate your fear but to understand and manage it, transforming it into a catalyst for your growth rather than being a barrier to your success.

Confidence, on the other hand, is the antidote to fear. It's the belief in your abilities, vision, and capacity to overcome challenges. Building confidence doesn't mean you won't experience fear, but ensures that fear won't control your decisions. Confidence comes from preparation, experience, and the mindset that every obstacle is an opportunity for you to learn and grow.

UNDERSTANDING AND MANAGING YOUR FEAR

To overcome your fear, you must first understand it. Fear can stem from the unknown and uncertainty about the future, your abilities, or the potential outcomes of your decisions. Acknowledging your fears is the first step in managing them. Ask yourself: What exactly am I afraid of? Is it the fear of failure, the fear of financial instability, or perhaps the fear of judgment from others?

Once you have identified your fears, you can address them systematically. Preparation is one of the most effective ways to reduce fear. The more prepared you are, the less intimidating the unknown becomes. This could mean developing a solid business plan, acquiring new skills, or seeking mentorship from experienced entrepreneurs.

Visualization is another powerful tool for managing fear. By visualizing yourself successfully navigating challenges and achieving your goal of breaking free from your 9-to-5, you create a mental roadmap that makes the journey seem less daunting. This mental rehearsal can significantly boost your confidence, allowing you to anticipate and prepare for potential obstacles.

BUILDING YOUR CONFIDENCE

Confidence is not an inherent trait; it's a skill that can be developed over time. One of the most effective ways to build confidence is by setting and achieving small, incremental goals. Each small victory reinforces your belief in your abilities and builds momentum toward larger achievements.

Self-awareness is also crucial in building your confidence. Understanding your strengths and weaknesses allows you to leverage what you're good at while seeking help or improvement in areas where you're less confident. This honest self-assessment can prevent the fear of inadequacy from holding you back.

Surrounding yourself with a supportive network is another essential element in building confidence. The encouragement and advice of others can help you maintain perspective and stay motivated, especially during challenging times. Whether it's friends, family, or fellow entrepreneurs, a strong support system will be invaluable.

REFRAMING FAILURE

One of the most significant fears for any entrepreneur is the fear of failure. However, failure is an inevitable part of your entrepreneurial journey. Rather than fearing failure, reframing it as a learning experience is important. Every setback provides valuable insights that can guide your future decisions.

Adopting a growth mindset is key to reframing your failure. This mindset views challenges and failures as opportunities to grow and improve rather than reflections of your abilities or worth. With a growth mindset, failure becomes a stepping stone to success rather than an insurmountable obstacle.

THE ROLE OF RESILIENCE

Resilience is the ability to bounce back from setbacks and is closely linked to fear and confidence. The more resilient you are, the better equipped you'll be to face your fears and recover from failures. Resilience can be developed by maintaining a positive outlook, staying adaptable, and focusing on your long-term goals even when facing short-term challenges.

CULTIVATING A CONFIDENT MINDSET

A confident mindset embraces challenges, remains optimistic, and sees setbacks as temporary. To cultivate this mindset, practice gratitude and positive self-talk. Celebrate your achievements, no matter how small, and remind yourself of your past successes when facing new challenges.

Mindfulness and meditation can also play a significant role in building confidence. These practices help you stay present, reduce anxiety, and maintain a clear, focused mind. Regularly setting aside time for mindfulness or meditation can strengthen your ability to manage stress and approach challenges with a calm, confident demeanor.

CONCLUSION: EMBRACING THE JOURNEY

Overcoming fear and building confidence are essential for any entrepreneur. While fear is a natural part of stepping into the unknown, it doesn't have to hold you back. By understanding your fears, preparing for challenges, and building confidence through small successes, you can transform fear into a driving force for growth and achievement.

Remember, confidence is not about being fearless; it's about facing your fears with the belief that you have the power to overcome them. As you continue your journey to *Break Free from Your 9-to-5*, embrace each challenge as an opportunity to grow, and let your confidence guide you toward success.

If you would like my help with this, start by taking the Take Control of Your Life assessment at...

EMPOWER

4

THE 5 STEPS TO YOUR FREEDOM

FrEEdom

EMBRACE

EMPOWER

EMBARK

EVOLVE

ENLIGHTEN

FOLLOW YOUR PATH

EMBRACE. EMPOWER. EMBARK. EVOLVE. ENLIGHTEN.

These important steps are 5 strategies to take you through your journey of breaking free from your 9-to-5 to reaching your frEEdom and being self-employed.

Embrace your childhood dreams and transform them into reality. Overcome your pressures and insecurities. Dare yourself to be who you truly are. Build your self-esteem and confidence; find that passion and twinkle in your eyes so you can make a difference in your life and the lives of others.

Empower yourself in this fast-paced world. It can be difficult to stay mindful of your goals and make positive changes to help you become your best self. Empowering yourself by allowing yourself to make some enhancements in your life for your highest good is an important step in achieving personal growth and becoming the fullest version of yourself possible. Taking the time to invest in yourself and your goals allows you to better align your life with your purpose and continue striving to live a meaningful and fulfilling life.

Embark on a positive, proactive path, taking small but meaningful steps with purpose and passion, keeping your goal/destination in mind.

Evolve with a quantum mind-shift, a spiritual, subconscious energy, and physical transformation.

Enlighten those around you by making a difference and shining your light on someone else's dimming candle.

It's *your* time to **embrace** who you are, **empower** your inner change agent, **embark** on a positive, proactive journey of **evolving** through a quantum mind shift and subconscious, energetic, and physical transformation, and emerge on your path with passion and purpose, ready to **enlighten** others as you live well, feel well, and look great.

Let's expand on these 5 steps to your transformation.

EMBRACE

Embrace your opportunities; they can be your stepping stones to greatness. Embrace your physical self and live life to your fullest capacity. Embrace the past and prepare for the future.

It is so important to embrace who you are and your dreams, no matter what stage of life you are in.

Your childhood dreams may have changed over time, but that doesn't mean you can't still strive to make them happen. It is important to surround yourself with people who support you and encourage you to be who you are and pursue your dreams. That twinkle in your eyes and passion for your life and dreams can be empowering. It is never too late to make your dreams come true.

So, embrace who you are and make your dreams come true. By taking the time to appreciate who you are and recognizing your strengths, you can gain a greater understanding of yourself and your worth. Finding ways to embrace who you are is important to living a fulfilling and meaningful life.

Here are some tips to help you along the way.

- Celebrate your successes and accomplishments, no matter how small they may be.
- Take time to recognize and appreciate your hard work and dedication to achieving your goals.
- Spend time with people who love and appreciate you for who you are.
- Spend time with people who care about and understand you and make you feel valued and appreciated.
- Remind yourself of your positive qualities.
- Take time to reflect on the qualities that make you unique and special.
- Take pride in the things that make you who you are.
- Take risks. Push yourself out of your comfort zone and take on new challenges. Trying new things can help you discover new aspects of yourself and your strengths.
- Practice self-care. Take time for yourself and invest in activities that help you relax and recharge. Doing things that make you happy—such as reading a book,

walking, or taking a yoga class—can help you stay focused and centered.

- Find your purpose. Ask yourself what matters to you and what you want to achieve in life. Reflecting and exploring your purpose can help you stay motivated and focused on your goals.
- Surround yourself with positive affirmations. Spend time reading positive quotes, writing down your thoughts in a journal, and listening to inspiring podcasts.

These activities can help you stay focused and motivated. By taking the time to appreciate who you are and recognizing your strengths, you can gain a greater understanding of yourself and your worth.

THINGS YOU EMBRACE

1. What are your greatest talents or strengths?

_____

_____

2. What activities or hobbies bring you the most joy and fulfillment?

_____

_____

3. What values do you embrace, and how do they impact your actions and decisions?

_____

_____

4. What is your definition of success, and how do you measure it?

_____

_____

5. What inspires or motivates you to pursue your passions and purpose?

_____

_____

6. What obstacles have you overcome in the past, and how have they shaped the person you are today?

_____

_____

7. What unique qualities or experiences have you had and embraced that set you apart from others?

_____

_____

8. What do you love most about yourself?

_____

_____

9. What do you embrace as your best qualities?

_____

_____

EMPOWER

Empower yourself (give yourself permission) to make positive changes and steps forward to follow your heart.

You must grant yourself permission to make positive changes and follow your heart. This is an incredibly important step in fostering growth and becoming successful. An outside source cannot grant empowerment. Instead, it must come from accepting an internal responsibility and embracing self-growth. Achieving success is so much more than reaching a desired outcome; it's, first and foremost, the journey of trusting and believing in yourself.

This empowerment is fed by the courage to make decisions that require discipline, concentration, and faith. It takes strength and emotional resilience to understand and nurture personal growth, even when the goal is unclear and the effort is daunting. Yet without it, self-actualization and happiness remain out of reach.

To acquire such a responsibility, building trust and faith within yourself is crucial. To gain that trust, be kind to yourself by loving your weaknesses and quirks; stay positive when times are rough. Dream big. Believe firmly. Strive for excellence no matter the cost.

This notion of empowerment is not viewed from an external viewpoint or society's boundaries. Instead, it is a form of internal love and understanding. Give yourself permission to make the needed adjustments and decisions. Let go of what doesn't serve you anymore and make space for beautiful, new possibilities.

Reflect, meditate, and practice deciphering between real and false desires as they arise. Make sure to take calculated risks and never doubt the power of your capabilities. Know that with trust in yourself comes rewards and personal growth. And follow your heart—always. The courage to make positive changes will allow you to unlock new doors. Strive to keep yourself on this quest and never let go of the wheel.

Empowerment is self-satisfying and essential for success. With internal trust and faith, you can gain the strength to alter your course and follow your heart to reach your highest potential. Give yourself permission. You are capable, and you are ready for anything.

Empower your inner change agent. Empower yourself to make small changes for big differences in your mindset, energy, and image.

Empower your evolution with persistence, bounce-back ability, and self-confidence. Dream big, think big, do big! Be the best and at the top of your game; stand up for who you are, and don't settle for mediocrity.

Empower yourself and others to be all they can be. And, in the process, reach mind-blowing levels of success.

BROADEN YOUR SELF-EMPOWERMENT AWARENESS

1. What are your biggest obstacles/challenges?

_____

_____

2. Can you identify the #1 thing holding you back from achieving your wildest dreams?

_____

_____

3. What would you do today to move forward if that #1 thing didn't exist?

_____

_____

EMBARK

Embark on your journey of self-discovery, reevaluation, alignment, or realignment with your core values, true self, beliefs, and desires.

Journeying through life can often feel like a winding path with many forks and unexpected turns. You may find yourself standing at an unfamiliar crossroads, unsure of which direction to take. As you venture forward, engaging in a journey of self-discovery, reevaluation, and realignment can be beneficial. Self-discovery helps you better understand yourself, allowing you to make decisions and progress forward more intentionally and clearly. By exploring your beliefs, values, motivations, and desires, you can uncover a deeper, more meaningful understanding of who you are and how to live your life.

One of the greatest gifts of a journey of self-discovery and reevaluation is learning to trust yourself and follow your intuition. This often involves slowing down and consciously deepening your relationship with yourself. You can do this through meditation, journaling, and spending time intentionally reflecting. When engaged in such practices, you open yourself up to listen to and trust your inner voice and move with it rather than against it. You can begin to recognize and value the innate wisdom that resides within.

Self-discovery and reevaluation also allow you to better understand your emotions. You can become motivated to work toward personal growth, healing, and transforming your inner self. You can become aware of your coping mechanisms and defense mechanisms to develop a healthier and more adaptive relationship to your emotions. You can empower yourself to learn from your emotions rather than letting your emotions control you.

One of the most powerful aspects of a journey of self-discovery and reevaluation is that it allows you to unleash your creative potential. With increased self-awareness, you can nurture skills and abilities. You can explore your passions, values, and interests and be brave enough to manifest your ideas and share your creations with the world.

Embarking on a journey of self-discovery can be a potent source of strength and growth. It builds your self-confidence and allows you to lead a more authentic life. You learn to listen to and trust your intuition, work with your emotions, and unlock your creative potential. As you stand at the crossroads of life, you can invite yourself to embark on a self-discovery journey and explore, learn, and uncover a greater understanding of yourself.

Embark on a positive, proactive, healthy journey. Evolve through shifting your choices and habits and emerge with passion and purpose, ready to enlighten others as you live well and feel and look great. Together, let's build a beautiful life for you.

EMBARK ON YOUR JOURNEY

1. What does it mean to you to embark on a journey of self-discovery?

2. How can a mind shift support your transition from employee to entrepreneur as you *Break Free from Your 9-to-5?*

3. How can you manage self-doubt and uncertainty when embarking on your new venture?

4. As you embark on your journey, what steps can you take to evolve your mindset and embrace the challenges of entrepreneurship?

5. What role does perseverance play in your process of embarking on an entrepreneurial journey?

6. How can you use the lessons learned during this phase to inform and inspire your continued growth as an entrepreneur?

7. What advice would you give to someone who is just starting to consider embarking on their entrepreneurial journey?

_____

_____

8. How will you build a support network to help you through the ups and downs of your entrepreneurial journey?

_____

_____

EVOLVE

The concept of evolving with a quantum mind shift is one of self-transformation, driven by a desire to navigate life at a higher level of awareness. A quantum mind shift involves a spiritual, subconscious, energetic, and physical transformation that leads to a deeper understanding of the work that lies beyond the bounds of the physical world. It is a shift in perception of life and reality on a deep, intrinsic level that requires you to look at life in a new way.

At the spiritual level, evolving with a quantum mind shift involves renewing one's inner spiritual growth. This inspires a journey of discovery that deepens the connection to a higher power while allowing the inner creative force, intuition, and soul's song to be more clearly heard. In essence, it is an inner re-awakening and acknowledgment that our divine spark, the part of us connected to everything, exists and needs to be nurtured and embraced.

At the subconscious level, a quantum mind shift is about understanding the autobiographical and adaptable nature of your beliefs and behavior patterns that tie you to your past. It is also about making changes that can lead to remapping your inner landscape and more creative thinking, contributing to your evolution. In addition, it encompasses an understanding of the need to break past limitations, bring the shadow self out of hiding, and become more conscious of and informed by sources of wisdom you weren't previously aware of.

At the energetic and physical level, a quantum mind shift requires you to undergo a molecular transformation and re-tune your energetic body to align with higher vibrations. This is accompanied by a commitment to a physical practice, the release of bodily toxins, and the development of a connection with one's physical form. At its core, the shift involves an accelerated movement from the cognitive level of the physical, mental, and emotional body toward a level of transformation where old thought patterns and behaviors are replaced with new ones more rooted in a higher quality of life.

Evolving with a quantum mind shift requires you to embrace your evolution and take the necessary steps toward personal transformation. Ultimately, this kind of shift promises a life where you experience fulfillment through the integration of your inner power, creativity, and spirit. It is a means of shifting your perspective to allow you to master the unknown while igniting your internal capacity to transform.

YOUR EVOLUTION JOURNEY

1. What inspired you to want to transition from employee to entrepreneur and *Break Free from Your 9-to-5*? Was it a personal desire or something external, like a change in your career or life?

———————————————————————————

———————————————————————————

2. What are some of the challenges you anticipate facing during this evolution? How have you prepared or planned to prepare for those challenges?

———————————————————————————

———————————————————————————

3. What personal obstacles will you need to tackle to successfully evolve? How do you plan to approach those obstacles?

_____

_____

4. What kind of support system will you need during this process? Who in your life can you turn to for help and advice?

_____

_____

5. What kind of mindset do you need to successfully evolve?

_____

_____

6. What steps have you taken or do you plan to take to gradually evolve and transition from your current role to pursuing entrepreneurship full-time?

_____

_____

7. Are there any specific skills, knowledge, or resources you need to acquire to succeed as an entrepreneur? If so, what are they? How do you plan to acquire them?

_____

_____

8. How will you measure your progress and success as you move along this entrepreneurial journey? What specific goals or milestones have you set for yourself? How will you know when you have arrived?

_____

_____

9. What is your ultimate vision for your life as an entrepreneur? How does it align with your values and goals?

_____

_____

ENLIGHTEN

In today's world, there is arguably nothing more valuable than enlightening those around you and making a difference in someone else's life. By being an uplifting force and an example of what is possible, we can have a lasting impact on the people in our lives and the lives of those around us. When you understand the ripple effect of kindness and all the ways it can spread, you are empowered to be the light to someone else's dimming candle.

At its core, enlightening and making a difference are core values that holistically strengthen our society. When we help bring people out of darkness, we open the door for more positive experiences for ourselves and others. Enlightening others also involves encouraging them to take risks and push boundaries, challenging our habits and beliefs. This growth sets the foundation for healthier lifestyles, richer relationships, and a more compassionate collective.

Being a light for those around you doesn't always require complex and heroic efforts. Often, it is the smallest gestures that make the biggest difference. Offering your friendship, listening to their experiences, and simply lending a shoulder for them to lean on can offer a great source of comfort and healing. Enlightening those around you does not have to take the form of grand gestures or large-scale endeavors. It is the small things that have the most significant impact on your communities and their lives.

Giving others a light in their darkness can have unimaginably far-reaching effects. It is a remarkable way to brighten someone's day. Whether it's a conversation, a smile, or an encouraging word, putting forth an effort to support others can instill purpose and ambition in their lives. Through a kind and thoughtful approach, you can remind those around you that they are worthy of love, support, and the opportunity to succeed.

Enlightening those around you and making a difference is at the heart of leaving a legacy. As you strive to be a source of hope and optimism, it is essential to understand the power of your everyday actions—no matter how small. Even a single candle can light the way for others and show that we can move mountains together. By being a guiding light for those around you and offering them the opportunity to better their lives, you are laying the foundation for a brighter future for all of us.

ARE YOU READY TO ENLIGHTEN OTHERS?

1. How do you plan to uplift others with your new business?

_____

_____

2. In what ways will you give back to your customers and community?

_____

_____

3. Will you start a non-profit foundation? What are some of your ideas around this?

_____

_____

5

RECONNECTING WITH YOUR VISION AND PURPOSE

Create a life that feels good on the inside, not just one that looks good on the outside.

SETTING *YOUR* LIFE GOALS

As you embark on the journey from employee to entrepreneur and *Break Free from Your 9-to-5,* it's important to clearly understand what you want to achieve in life.

Setting goals and knowing what you want to accomplish can help you stay motivated and focused on your objectives. This chapter will explore the importance of setting life goals and some techniques to achieve them.

WHY SET LIFE GOALS?

Setting goals gives you direction and purpose. It helps you determine what is important in your life and maximizes your efforts toward achieving your dreams. Knowing what you want and where you want to go allows you to plan your actions in a way that is more efficient and effective. With a clear vision of your goals, you can work hard to achieve them and gain the sense of fulfillment that comes from the realization of your aspirations.

Setting life goals can also help you measure your progress. It is essential to track your progress if you want to achieve success. Without goals, you may feel like you're working hard but not making significant progress toward achieving anything. Having measurable goals allows you to track your progress and adjust your efforts accordingly.

HOW TO SET YOUR LIFE GOALS

To set your life goals, you must first consider what matters most to you.

- What do you want to achieve in life?
- What are your dreams?
- What do you want to be remembered for after you're gone?

These questions can help you identify what you truly want in life.

Once you've determined your priorities, it's time to set specific goals around them. These goals should be specific, measurable, achievable, relevant, and time-bound (SMART). Make sure your goals are not too general. With a goal that states, "I want to be successful," the level of success is difficult to measure.

Instead, set specific SMART goals, such as, "I want to start a successful digital marketing agency that generates six figures of income in one year."

Next, create an action plan. A plan will help you break down your goals into actionable steps. Personalizing your action plan and tailoring it to your needs, personality, and work style is important.

Finally, make sure your goals are written down and visible. Writing your goals down and placing them in a visible location can serve as a constant reminder of what you want to achieve. Setting life goals is critical to achieve success in any area of your life.

ENTREPRENEURSHIP

Transitioning from employee to entrepreneur and breaking free from your 9-to-5 can be scary. However, it has become more feasible in today's digital world. To successfully *Break Free from Your 9-to-5,* there are a few key considerations and steps to take.

> ➤ **Key 1:** One must carefully assess the risk involved in becoming an entrepreneur. Running a business requires extensive resources and commitment. It is important to be aware of the potential challenges and pitfalls that may arise. Risk assessment involves considering various

factors such as financial security, market and competitive dynamics, desired lifestyle, and levels of dedication. After the risk has been evaluated, it is important to develop a business plan that clearly outlines the goals and objectives of the new venture.

➤ **Key 2:** Consider the kind of business to launch and the target market. Business owners must identify the needs of their target audience and the industry in which they are trying to compete. In the process, you must research to gain insight into the industry's current and emerging trends and business practices, as well as the level of competition. Your business model can be crafted after conducting research and performing market analysis.

➤ **Key 3:** Besides the research and market analysis, entrepreneurs must find ways to manage the practical demands of running their new business. This includes creating a budget and managing expenses, establishing and maintaining relationships with suppliers, recruiting and training personnel, creating a marketing strategy, and staying informed about legal regulations and compliance.

➤ **Key 4:** The last key is using available resources to launch your business successfully. This includes accessing capital through bank loans, crowdfunding, and venture capital and deploying technology, such as mobile apps and online platforms, to increase reach and efficiency.

A motivated employee can successfully and confidently leap into entrepreneurship by using these key steps as a guide. This journey takes hard work and dedication. However, the transition to *Break Free from Your 9-to-5* can be successful with the right preparation and approach.

DEFINING YOUR GAP

How many assets do you have? How much did your budget indicate you needed available as a minimum to pay your bills? What upcoming big expenses—trips, vacations, saving for college for your kids—do you have?

What is your *why*? Does it match what you are doing and where you are on your journey right now? Where do you want to be?

When I started my journey from employee to entrepreneur, I worked full-time for someone else and part-time on my dreams and goals. I was so caught up in balancing my engineering career, my kid's activities, and my marriage, or lack thereof, that I found little time or energy to think about what I wanted out of life or how to get there. I had no vision for my life or my mission; I was trying to figure out my purpose. That's a big reason I'm sharing my experiences and suggestions with you: I know someone out there needs this.

1. What is your current skill set?

_____

_____

In my early corporate career, I started building a toolbox of communication, technology, leadership, and networking skills to advance that career. I looked at the next job level description and what was required. If I didn't have that skill set, I learned it or took a class and/or certification.

2. What courses, classes, certifications, personal development, professional development, business skills, communication skills, or customer service skills do you need to acquire?

_____

_____

3. What personal assets do you have?

_____

_____

4. Last but not least, how much money do you need to start
your business? Is there any capital involved?

_____

_____

BUILDING YOUR TOOL KIT OF SKILLS AND KNOWLEDGE

When deciding to *Break Free from Your 9-to-5*, one of the most
important things you need to do is build your tool kit of skills
and knowledge. While being an employee provides certain
skills and experience, there are many others that are critical
to successfully running your own business. In this chapter,
we'll explore some of the essential skills and knowledge every
entrepreneur needs in their tool kit.

1. **Financial Management**: As an entrepreneur, you'll be
   responsible for managing your business's finances. This
   includes creating budgets, managing cash flow, and
   handling taxes. It's important to understand accounting
   and finance to effectively manage your resources and
   make informed financial decisions.
2. **Sales and Marketing:** To be a successful entrepreneur,
   you need to know how to sell your product or service.
   This means understanding your market, identifying
   your target audience, and crafting compelling sales
   pitches. You also need to be able to effectively market
   your product or service using social media, advertising,
   and other marketing channels.

3. **Project Management:** Entrepreneurs need to be able to manage projects effectively, ensuring resources are being used efficiently and projects are completed on time and within budget. This includes developing project plans, identifying risks and roadblocks, and delegating tasks to team members.

4. **Leadership:** As an entrepreneur, you'll lead a team of employees or contractors. You need to be able to inspire and motivate them while setting clear expectations and holding them accountable. This requires excellent communication skills, the ability to delegate effectively, and the willingness to take responsibility for your team's work outcomes.

5. **Technical Skills:** Depending on the nature of your business, you may need technical skills in areas such as web development, software engineering, or graphic design. Even if you plan to hire others to handle these tasks, having a basic understanding of the technical aspects of your business will help you make informed decisions and communicate effectively with your team.

6. **Industry Knowledge:** Finally, it's important to have a deep understanding of the industry you're operating in. This includes knowing your competitors, staying up to date with the latest trends and innovations, and understanding the regulatory environment in which you operate.

By building your skills and knowledge tool kit, you'll be well-positioned to *Break Free from Your 9-to-5*. Take the time to identify areas where you may have gaps.

RATE YOURSELF

Who are you now, and who do you want to become? For me, it was transitioning back to my true, unapologetically authentic self at my core.

Rate each category to see where you are now and where you want to be. Rate yourself on a scale from 1 (low) to 10 (high).

	Where I Am	Where I Want to Be
Finances		
Lifestyle		
Physical		
Spiritual		
Time/Flexibility		
Relationships		
Self-Care		
Travel		

Identify the main thing holding you back from transitioning to and living your dream life. If that one thing didn't exist, what would you do today to move forward? What would the results look like?

Repeat often, "I am ready. I deserve the life of my dreams, on path, with purpose, and on my terms."

It's also important to know when you've achieved your goals. You must know how you define happiness and success. What does success look like to you?

There's also a gap many experience relating to a connection to their core values and beliefs that need realignment as part of this process.

- Do you have a list of core beliefs and values?

- Are you in alignment with them?

- Does your head match your heart and your core beliefs and values?

- Do you practice those things you are passionate about daily?

Energy with passion behind it radiates at a much higher energy and frequency level than without. The result is manifesting more in your life at a faster pace. The purpose of your journey is to overcome a trapped existence of your true self at your core.

Some important questions to ask yourself as you dive deeper into self-discovery include:

Until now, have you considered your career the career of a lifetime?	Yes	No
Is what you are currently doing what you went to school for?	Yes	No
Are you now ready to monetize your passions?	Yes	No

Are you aligned with your core values and beliefs regarding what you currently do for work?	Yes	No
Are you passionate about your current job?	Yes	No
Does what you do for work bring joy to you?	Yes	No

Identifying Your Core Values and Beliefs

The Importance of Identifying Your Core Values

Breaking free from your 9-to-5 is an exciting and rewarding journey. You'll soon be your own boss! You have the freedom to pursue your passion and create a business around it. However, with this newfound freedom comes the responsibility of making decisions that will greatly impact the success of your business. Identifying your core values is one of the most important steps to take when transitioning from employee to entrepreneur and breaking free from your 9-to-5

What are Core Values?

Core values are the *fundamental beliefs and principles that guide your decision-making process.* These values shape your character, influence your thoughts and actions, and help you maintain integrity in everything you do. They are the foundation of your personal and professional life. Your core values should always align with your business goals.

WHY ARE CORE VALUES IMPORTANT?

Identifying your core values when transitioning from employee to entrepreneur and breaking free from your 9-to-5 is crucial. Identifying your core values will help you make the right decisions when faced with difficult circumstances. Your core values will guide you in creating a business that represents who you are and reflects what you believe. Your core values will also help you establish a sense of purpose and direction, allowing you to differentiate yourself from your competitors and build a loyal customer base.

HOW TO IDENTIFY YOUR CORE VALUES

1. Reflect on your past experiences. Think about the moments in your life where you felt fulfilled and satisfied. What was it about those moments that gave you a sense of purpose and happiness? Identifying these experiences can help you identify the values and beliefs behind them.
2. Define your purpose. Ask yourself why you decided to become an entrepreneur. What drives you to wake up every day and work on your business? Write your purpose down and use it as a foundation to identify your core values.
3. Prioritize your values. Make a list of values that are important to you. Prioritize them based on their significance. Consider values such as honesty, integrity, compassion, creativity, innovation, and teamwork.
4. Test your values. Once you've identified your core values, test them by aligning them with your business goals. Do they support your vision and mission statements? Do they help guide your decision-making process? If

your core values don't align with your business goals, it's time to re-assess and make any necessary adjustments.

SUMMARY

Transitioning from employee to entrepreneur and breaking free from your 9-to-5 can be scary. Identifying your core values can help mitigate the risks and create a solid foundation for your business.

In the chart below, circle the values that resonate with who you are and what you stand for and align with you and your beliefs. Circle as many as you feel necessary.

Now, narrow it down to your 5 core values. These are the 5 pillars that define you.

Authenticity	Contribution	Happiness	Love	Power	Spirituality
Adventure	Curiosity	Honesty	Loyalty	Recognition	Stability
Authority	Determination	Influence	Openness	Religion	Success
Balance	Dignity	Innovation	Optimism	Reputation	Trustworthy
Beauty	Dedication	Integrity	Passion	Respect	Wealth
Bravery	Faith	Justice	Patience	Responsibility	Wisdom
Compassion	Family	Kindness	Peace	Security	
Citizenship	Friendship	Knowledge	Persistence	Self-Respect	
Community	Fun	Leadership	Playfulness	Service	

DISCOVERING YOUR WHY REQUIRES TAKING 3 STEPS:

1. Identifying your natural God-given gifts/talents.
2. Identifying the best vehicle for sharing your gifts/talents with the world.
3. Identifying the specific audience who will benefit most from your gifts/talents.

Most people will die without living their purpose.

My Why

My why is to build generational wealth and live, lead, and leave a legacy.

To show and inspire my adult kids and young grandkids that all things are possible, so:

- They have a positive role model leading the way.
- They learn and have instilled in them a good work ethic and how hard work and planning pay off.
- They can be self-sufficient.
- They can be positive role models for their kids and families.
- Together, we can create generational wealth.
- They know that if they can dream it, they can achieve it!

To repurpose my husband so we can live our lives outrageously with no limitations or boundaries and give freely to people and causes we are passionate about, so:

- We can show other couples how to communicate, dream, plan, and maximize each other's strengths so more couples see the possibilities and results of working and playing together.
- Families are thriving so they can be role models and positive influences in their communities.
- Fewer people are on food stamps and struggling.

- Anxiety, fear, and crime are diminished, and positivity and love prevail.

To help burnt-out women and men have hope and a road-map to get out of corporate and live their life on purpose and in alignment with their core values with a vision that pulls them to their greatness, so;

- They gain hope.
- They can fulfill their dreams.
- Their incredible, life-changing ideas can help others and improve the world.

WHY IT'S IMPORTANT FOR AN ENTREPRENEUR TO WRITE THEIR WHY

As an entrepreneur, getting caught up in the day-to-day tasks of running a business can be easy. There are emails to answer, invoices to send, meetings to attend, and so much more. However, one of the most important things any entrepreneur can do is write their business why.

✓ Why did they start their business?
✓ What is their purpose in doing what they do?

This may seem small, but it could mean the difference between success and failure.

➢ Having a clear sense of purpose can provide direction and motivation. It's easy to lose sight of what we're working toward when things get tough, as they inevitably do. Knowing your why can help you maintain focus and stay on track. It can also motivate you to keep going even when there seem to be too many obstacles in your way. When you know why you're doing something, it's easier to keep going—even when it's hard.

➤ A clear why can also help you make better decisions. When faced with a difficult choice, your purpose can guide you. If an opportunity aligns with your why, it's likely to be a good fit for your business. It might not be the best decision if it doesn't align with your purpose. A clear sense of purpose can help you make better decisions that align with your values and goals.

➤ Having a clear why can help you communicate your passion to others. As an entrepreneur, you will likely be doing something you're passionate about. However, if you can't articulate why you care about your business or your product, it's unlikely that others will get excited about it. Knowing your purpose can help you communicate your passion to others and get them excited about what you're doing.

➤ Finally, having a clear why can help you build a strong brand. Your purpose can serve as the foundation for your branding and marketing efforts. When you know what you stand for, creating a brand that reflects those values is easier. Customers are more likely to connect with a brand that has a clear sense of purpose and values.

In summary, as an entrepreneur, it's important to take the time to write your why. Knowing your purpose can provide direction and motivation and help you make better decisions, communicate your passion to others, and build a strong brand. Take the time now to do this below.

It's Time to Write Your WHY

_____

WHO AM I, WHAT DO I DO WHO DO I SERVE

Vision

Mission

Core Values

Strategic Goals

Target Market

6

BELIEF, FAITH, AND VISUALIZATION

let your *Faith* be bigger than your *Fear*

B elief and faith are powerful elements of human life that you can harness to help you transition out of corporate life and *Break Free from Your 9-to-5.*

- Belief is defined as having a strong conviction that something exists, is true, and is worth achieving.
- Faith is defined as complete trust or confidence in someone or something.

Having a strong belief in yourself and trusting your path can give you the confidence to walk away from some of the perceived safety corporate life can offer and take a leap of faith toward a new, more grounded state of life.

In today's world, the idea of transitioning out of corporate life to pursue a more fulfilling path is becoming increasingly common. There is a strong desire to find personal freedom and an opportunity to express one's true potential. This requires taking a leap of faith, believing in yourself, and trusting your path will lead you to something greater.

Belief can be a strong motivator for you to take this leap of faith, whether the belief is in yourself or a higher power or purpose. It's the assurance that comes from having a strong conviction that something is true and worth pursuing. It is the desire to discover the true potential you possess. By believing the future can be filled with hope, joy, and fulfillment, you can find the courage to move away from the confinement of corporate life and embrace an unknown future.

In your journey from breaking free from your 9-to-5, believing in yourself is the first and most important step. It is a prerequisite for success. Without it, your journey becomes difficult and, eventually, insurmountable.

WHY BELIEF IS CRUCIAL

Belief is crucial in the journey from employee to entrepreneur. Without a deep-seated belief in your ability to succeed, you will likely struggle with self-doubt, fear, and hesitation. These emotions can hold you back from taking risks, trying new things, and reaching your potential. Belief is the rocket fuel that propels us forward, enabling us to take fearless action toward our goals.

STANDING IN YOUR POWER

Believing in self is not just a mental state; it's also a physical state. You stand with confidence, clarity, and conviction when you believe in yourself. Outside opinions, criticism, or self-doubt do not easily sway you. You understand your strengths and limitations and are willing to take calculated risks to achieve your goals.

OVERCOMING SELF-LIMITING BELIEFS

Self-limiting beliefs are beliefs you hold that restrict you in some way. They may be rooted in past experiences, societal expectations, or familial ideologies. These beliefs can sap your confidence and hold you back from pursuing your dreams. We will discuss strategies to help you overcome self-limiting beliefs and cultivate a positive mindset that nurtures your journey to entrepreneurship.

Belief is the cornerstone of success in the world of entrepreneurship. A deep-seated belief in yourself and your ability to succeed will help you stay motivated, overcome obstacles, and achieve your dreams of entrepreneurship. By standing in your power and developing a positive mindset, you can leverage your belief to create a life and career that is fulfilling, empowering, and inspiring.

FAITH

Faith is the next step in this journey. You must trust in your decisions and the path you are taking. You must trust that the result will be greater than the sum of its parts. It is the understanding that sometimes the journey can be challenging, and although it won't always lead to the desired outcome, you must have the willingness to ride out the highs and lows to reach a more grounded state. Having faith in oneself, faith in the present, and faith in the future can give you the courage to make difficult decisions and trust the changes you are making will lead to something greater.

Belief and faith are powerful forces that can be tapped into to help you transition out of corporate life. The courage for you to take a daring leap of faith and trust that the path being taken will achieve something beyond the mundane comes from having a strong belief in yourself and trusting in the unlimited potential you hold within. Faith gives you the strength to stay the course, battle the doubts and fears, and never give up on yourself.

AVOIDING IMPOSTER SYNDROME

Entrepreneurship is a challenging path. It requires a lot of hard work, perseverance, and self-belief. The journey of an entrepreneur is filled with ups and downs. As an entrepreneur, it is not uncommon for you to experience moments of self-doubt and insecurity. One common experience entrepreneurs face at some point in their careers is imposter syndrome.

Imposter syndrome is a psychological phenomenon where individuals doubt their abilities and accomplishments, feeling like frauds despite having evidence of their success. For you as an entrepreneur, this experience can be particularly challenging because you are often taking risks, venturing into unknown territory, and facing many uncertainties. Imposter syndrome can be debilitating and negatively affect your confidence, productivity, and decision-making abilities.

One of the reasons entrepreneurs may experience imposter syndrome is the pressure to always succeed. Entrepreneurs are often viewed as go-getters who have all the answers and the confidence to make things happen. However, the reality is that entrepreneurs face many failures and setbacks along the way. When entrepreneurs experience failure, they may question their skills and abilities, leading to imposter syndrome.

Another cause of imposter syndrome for entrepreneurs is the comparison trap. In today's world, it's easy to look at other entrepreneurs who have achieved great success and feel inadequate in comparison. Social media platforms like LinkedIn and Twitter can exacerbate this feeling as entrepreneurs are bombarded with posts showcasing others' accomplishments, making it easy to feel like they don't measure up.

Finally, entrepreneurship can be a lonely journey. Entrepreneurs often work long hours; the pressure to succeed can be isolating. It's common for entrepreneurs to feel like they're going through the journey alone, amplifying feelings of imposter syndrome.

There are many negative effects of imposter syndrome on entrepreneurs' lives, including anxiety, depression, burnout, and decreased self-esteem. However, there are ways to overcome imposter syndrome and regain confidence and self-assurance.

One way to combat imposter syndrome is to remind yourself of your achievements and successes. Keeping a list of accomplishments can be a powerful tool to remind you of your abilities and build your self-esteem. You must surround yourself with supportive people, including mentors, friends, and family members, who can provide encouragement, support, and advice.

Another way to overcome imposter syndrome is to recognize and address the negative self-talk that often accompanies these feelings.

Which brings us to...

THE POWER OF AFFIRMATIONS

As you begin your journey of breaking free from your 9-to-5, positive affirmations are one powerful tool you can utilize. Positive affirmations are statements you repeat to yourself that help focus your mind on the outcome you desire. They help you cultivate a positive, optimistic mindset, which is essential for success as an entrepreneur.

The power of positive affirmations lies in their ability to shape your thoughts and beliefs. When you consistently repeat positive affirmations, you reprogram your subconscious mind to think positively and focus on your goals. This can lead to increased confidence, motivation, and creativity, all critical factors in entrepreneurship.

To effectively use positive affirmations, start by identifying a few key affirmations that resonate with you. These statements should focus on your strengths, goals, and vision for your future. Examples of positive affirmations include:

- I am confident in my abilities.
- I have everything I need to succeed.
- Every obstacle is an opportunity for growth.
- Success is within my reach.

Once you have chosen your affirmations, it is crucial for you to repeat them consistently. You can write them down and read them aloud every morning or before bed. You can also record them and listen to them while you drive or exercise.

Positive affirmations alone will not guarantee success. You must also take action toward your goals and remain dedicated to your vision. However, positive affirmations can help you maintain a positive mindset during the ups and downs of entrepreneurship. They can also help you achieve your goals.

To summarize, positive affirmations are a powerful tool to help you on your journey from breaking free from your 9-to-5. By consistently repeating positive statements focusing on your strengths and goals, you can train your mind to think positively and stay motivated. As you continue your journey, remember that anything is possible with hard work and a positive mindset.

VISUALIZATION

The process of making a career change can be scary. With so much to consider, making an educated decision about an entirely new job can be difficult. Fortunately, several visual tools are available that can help make the decision-making process simpler and more manageable. Visualization techniques allow individuals to 'see' the different options and help them determine which career would be the best fit for them.

The concept of visualization is rooted in the belief that a person can learn and understand complex data better when presented in a visual format. Visualization techniques can be used to break down complex career data, such as job titles, necessary training, required skills and experience, salary expectations, and job satisfaction ratings. These data points are far easier to process when presented in a visual format. This also helps you make decisions that are more informed and better suited to your specific needs and interests.

Visualization techniques can also be used to quickly identify patterns in job data.

For example, an individual may be able to compare their current job against another job they are considering and instantly note the differences in necessary skills, salary, and job satisfaction. This can help the individual form an idea of what the new job might feel like. It can also help give a better idea of the lifestyle changes that might be required to successfully transition to the new career.

Other visualization techniques include using mind maps, concept maps, and graphing tools to analyze career options.

- ✔ Mind maps are useful because they help break down the components of different career paths and make connections between them.
- ✔ Concept maps allow a person to visualize a career path from start to finish, allowing them to understand what intervals are necessary to move up in their career.
- ✔ Graphs are used to identify trends in job satisfaction or salary among different groups, which can further inform career decisions.

Visualization techniques offer a way to gain insight into the many aspects of a possible career path. By breaking down complex job data into tangible, easily digestible images and patterns, they allow you to confidently make decisions and create a career path tailored to your interests, skills, and goals.

MIND MAPPING

Mind mapping your transition from employee to entrepreneur and breaking free from your 9-to-5 is a great way to plan a successful transition and develop a successful career in entrepreneurship. It allows you to break down the necessary steps to reach your desired destination. It also means that you can start to plan a timeline that will enable you to track your progress and take action when necessary. As an employee, you may often feel trapped and without options. By creating a mind map, you can remove this feeling of helplessness and empower yourself with a visual representation of the many options available and the steps you can take to achieve them.

To begin, you can use mind mapping to evaluate your current skill sets, interests, needs, and ambitions to identify what areas can be developed to successfully transition to entrepreneurship. You can then use mind mapping to list possible ideas, resources, and other steps that can help you reach your goal. This might include researching industries and markets, looking into potential business models, finding customer types, and evaluating different strategies. This way, you can identify the best opportunities to make your new venture thrive and succeed.

Once you have created your mind map and identified what you need to do to make the transition to entrepreneurship, you can use the same technique to plot your journey.

For example, you can map out the different stages of your transition by plotting a timeline of tasks that need to be completed and objectives that need to be achieved. This will ensure you are making steady progress toward your goals and that you can easily identify when any changes need to be made or any additional resources or time need to be added.

Mind mapping can also be a great tool for developing creative thinking and problem-solving skills, which are essential for any successful entrepreneur. By using mind maps to map your journey, you can visualize your options and understand the possibilities available. This will allow you to consider different solutions and approaches to find the best one for your situation.

Overall, mind mapping is a great way to make the transition from employee to entrepreneur. It can give you the focus and direction you need to build your successful business venture. By evaluating your skills and interests, mapping your journey, and encouraging creative thinking, you can ensure you are well-equipped to move forward to a successful future as an entrepreneur.

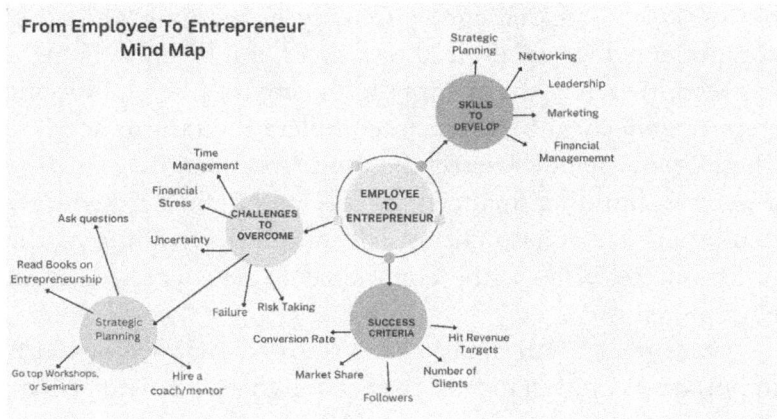

From Employee To Entrepreneur
Mind Map

Concept Mapping

Creating a concept map for transitioning from employee to entrepreneur and breaking free from your 9-to-5 can be important in initiating your creative journey. Concept mapping is an effective tool that can help organize your thoughts, develop ideas and connections between concepts, and lead to powerful decisions that can help you succeed as an entrepreneur.

A concept map organizes your ideas and their relationships in a graphical format. The concept map elements represent the components of the entrepreneurial journey to start your business. By creating this document, you can focus on specific tasks, activities, and areas that are important in transitioning from employee to entrepreneur.

The first step in developing your concept map is identifying your main goal. It could be starting a small business, launching a product, or even working at home. Once your goal is in place, you must determine what needs to be done to reach your goal. You then list the major tasks and activities needed to achieve that goal. These could include developing a business plan, researching the industry, networking, and other components that would lead to a successful business launch.

Within each of the major tasks or activities, several specific steps may need to be taken to complete the task or activity. These could include researching products or services, creating a website, building financial models, and defining the target market. This can help create a deeper understanding of the tasks and activities to be completed to be successful as an entrepreneur.

Once the activities, tasks, and steps are mapped out, it is important to understand the connections between them. Many entrepreneurial activities go hand-in-hand and will require different actions to be taken simultaneously.

For example, creating a website and building financial models must be done simultaneously to launch a business effectively. Identifying and understanding how connections impact each other can help guide your decision-making and ensure the required activities and tasks are done correctly.

Last, it is important to consider the timeline associated with the activities. Concept mapping allows you to understand the concept and provides a timeline for when the activities should be completed. This will help you track progress, organize your project, and set achievable goals.

Creating a content or concept map for your transition to entrepreneurship can help identify the tasks and activities involved in launching a business and provide a timeline for achieving your goals.

Content Map: Employee to Entrepreneur

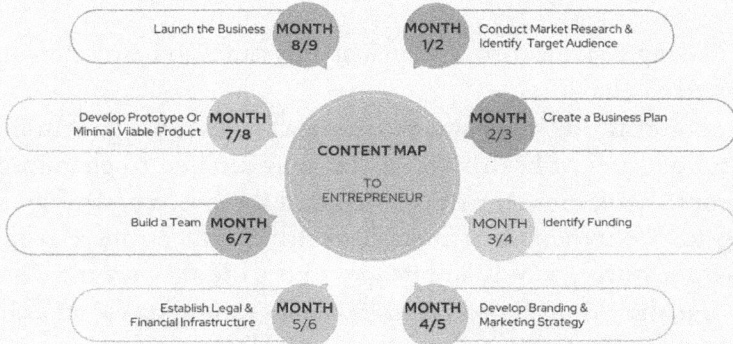

Launch the Business | **MONTH 8/9**

MONTH 1/2 | Conduct Market Research & Identify Target Audience

Develop Prototype Or Minimal Viiable Product | **MONTH 7/8**

CONTENT MAP TO ENTREPRENEUR

MONTH 2/3 | Create a Business Plan

Build a Team | **MONTH 6/7**

MONTH 3/4 | Identify Funding

Establish Legal & Financial Infrastructure | **MONTH 5/6**

MONTH 4/5 | Develop Branding & Marketing Strategy

DAILY VISUALIZATION

Daily visualization techniques can be a powerful tool for personal development, allowing you to create positive habits, reach goals, and increase your overall well-being. By utilizing various visualization techniques, you can create an image of your desired reality and then program your conscious and unconscious mind to achieve it.

Visualization techniques such as guided imagery and affirmations can be used to help you stay focused on desired outcomes.

- ✔ With guided imagery, you create a detailed, vivid mental image of something you want, such as a promotion or a healthier lifestyle.

✔ Conversely, affirmations involve repeating positive phrases about yourself and your goals to reprogram your subconscious mind.

Using visualization and visual aids can also help reinforce positive behaviors.

For example, a person pursuing a weight-loss goal might hang pictures of healthy meals in their kitchen to encourage them to cook more nutritious dishes. Likewise, a person looking to strengthen their mental health might create a vision board featuring words and images of the life they want to live.

Finally, visualizing daily tasks, such as studying for an exam or completing a project, can be a powerful time-management tool. Seeing the tasks laid out head-on can help break them down into smaller, more manageable chunks of work. It can also give you a better understanding of how much time and effort each task requires, allowing you to adjust your approach to be more efficient.

Daily visualization techniques can have a dramatic impact on personal development. Using these tools to program your conscious and unconscious mind can create positive habits, reach goals, and set yourself up for success.

Vision Casting

One of my favorite ways to visualize is by writing a letter to my future self. I set aside alone time in a peaceful, grounding environment. I begin with a blank piece of paper. First, I write down the 6 pillars of my life. These are family/friends, faith, finances, fun, leadership, and travel. These 6 pillars are the areas of my life where I want to grow, manifest greatness, and see the manifestation of my dreams.

Close your eyes and imagine your perfect life, including your perfect place to live and work life. Think about it in every detail: colors, designs, smells, sounds, the people you will be serving, the people you will be hanging around with, and the things you will be doing.

It's time to write a letter to your future self, 1 to 5 years from now. Throw those hopes, dreams, and goals out into the universe so you can begin to manifest them.

Remember to include your wildest dreams. If failure was not an option, what one thing could you do today to move closer to your life by design?

Writing this on paper has so much power; it sets the universe in motion to hear and answer. I do this yearly. One of my letters is for 1 year out; the other is for 5 years out. So many things come true year after year. I write my letters in the present tense; I suggest you do the same.

Dream big! Don't hold back!

Here is an excerpt from one of my longer, more detailed letters.

"Dear Phyllis Marlene,

I couldn't be prouder of how far I have come on my journey from employee to entrepreneur! It's now 2028, 5 years since I decided to take that leap of faith, with some hard work thrown in, to achieve personal freedom as an entrepreneur and successful business owner.

From embracing who I am at my core to empowering my evolution and embarking on my journey of self-discovery, to evolving into my true, best, and highest self, then going on to enlighten others with my gifts and talents and new products and services—what a journey it has been from inception to fruition! The lives I have begun to change are only the tip of the iceberg to the millions of lives I *will* change and the global impact I will have.

As I begin to get *paychecks of the heart* for all those I've helped, the monetary paychecks are also rolling in. Now, it's time to make some long-awaited upgrades and enhancements to my family's lives and my life.

Our new dream home on the beach is being built in Florida. It will also be a multi-use structure serving as a healing, retreat, and training center. I'm so excited to have the vehicle, products, services, and a place to serve so many who need and want it.

I can see it clearly now: a 3-story, modern, luxurious home with ocean-facing balconies on every level and 7 guest rooms painted in pastel coastal colors of purples, blues, and beiges. Our third-floor, penthouse-style living space with a master bathroom comes complete with an endless shower and the luxurious stone tile we've been waiting to arrive.

My kitchen has beautiful recycled glass countertops and an island that is perfect for entertaining. I'm always going with the lean, green options.

Those are just a few of my favorite details. I am looking forward to completing my home and having my morning coffee on one of the balconies and then a glass of wine while watching the sunset in the evening.

I have to pinch myself to make sure this is real. One of my favorite things is the freedom and flexibility I now have to spend precious time with my kids and grandkids and having the money to travel and see the 7 Wonders of the World.

Now, it's your turn.

EMBARK

7

TURNING YOUR PASSIONS INTO PROFIT

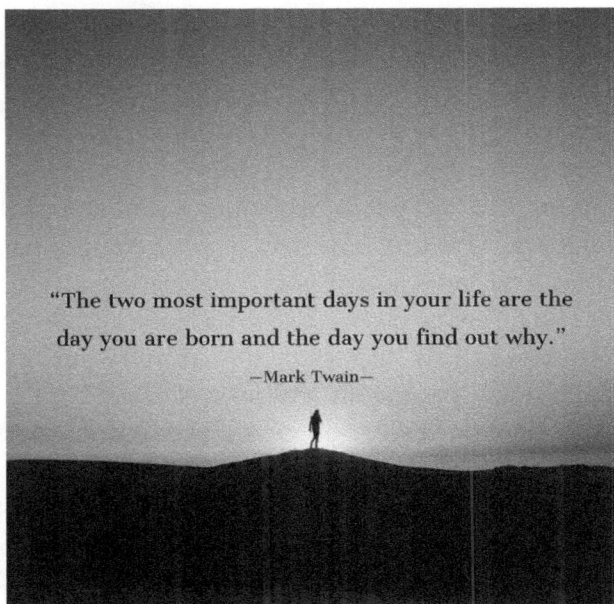

"The two most important days in your life are the
day you are born and the day you find out why."
—Mark Twain—

The world we live in today is full of opportunities.
Many people have turned their dreams and passions
into successful businesses. Will *you* be the next one?

It is possible to turn your passions into profit. But how do you go about doing this?

In this chapter, we will explore all these questions and more.

First, it is important to understand that turning your passion into profit is not an easy task. It requires a lot of hard work, dedication, and sacrifice. However, the journey becomes much more enjoyable and fulfilling if you are passionate.

What is your passion? What is it that gets you excited and keeps you motivated? This is perhaps the most crucial question you need to answer before embarking on your journey from employee to entrepreneur and breaking free from your 9-to-5. Your passion is what will drive you through the tough times and keep you focused on your goal.

Once you have identified your passion, you need to ask yourself if it has the potential to be turned into a profitable business. Is there a market for what you want to offer? Are there people willing to pay for your product or service? These are important questions you must answer.

Assuming you have identified your passion and confirmed there is a market for it, the next step is to start exploring the various business models that could work for you. There are countless business models out there, from e-commerce to freelance services. It is important to take your time and find a model that suits your skills and interests.

Once you have settled on a business model, it is time to start planning. This includes everything from creating a business plan and setting up a legal structure to developing a marketing strategy and identifying potential funding sources. This planning phase is crucial; it lays the foundation for the success of your business.

As you build your business, it is important to remember that it will take time to grow. Rome wasn't built in a day; your business won't be either. Don't expect overnight success.

Instead, focus on taking small steps daily to move your business forward.

One of the most important things you can do as you aspire to *Break Free From Your 9-to-5* is to seek mentors and advisors who can offer guidance and support. Joining entrepreneurial networks can be a great way to do this.

Let's design a blueprint for your life of EEs (ease). This is an excellent way to ensure a life rich with meaning and purpose.

You must be crystal clear about what you want. Throw it out to the universe. *Feel* into it. See it. Believe it. Smell it. Taste it. Start acting and doing the things you would do as if you had arrived.

What is included in what you want?

- ➤ Financial freedom?
- ➤ Work-life balance?
- ➤ A more harmonious life?
- ➤ Self-fulfillment?
- ➤ Time-money freedom?
- ➤ Flexibility?
- ➤ An unbounded life?
- ➤ More you time?
- ➤ Life on your terms?
- ➤ Your wildest dreams to come true?
- ➤ To have freedom as you define it?
- ➤ To live your life to the fullest with passion, purpose, intent, and a vision that pulls you to greatness?

Life is short. It's time to do what you love.

I'm passionate about showing others how to have a life of EEs—to be, do, and have more. I've been there. I will keep sharing with you the things you can start to do to begin your journey of being who you are at your core and who you were meant to be.

Are You Ready to *Break Free from Your 9-to-5*?

If your *why* is strong enough, you'll figure out the *how*. Your *why* will fuel you until you reach your destination.

In Chapter 5, you wrote your why. Your why should make you go over, under, around, and through any obstacles in your way. Your why should *drive* you. Your why should make you *cry*. Your why is not only for *what* you want, but it also includes *why* you want these things, so... Fill in the blanks.

With your why, you will step out in faith and follow through with great execution while developing a vision that *pulls* you.

Let's start with, "What's your thing?"

It's at the intersection of:

1) What lights you up
2) Your why
3) What you're good at
4) What problems you can solve and get paid for

Think back to when you've gotten results for people.

➤ For me, it was teaching makeup. I showed business-women how to do their makeup so they highlighted their natural features, brightened their eyes, showed off their smiles, looked professional, and let their inner beauty and energy shine.
➤ I also showed people how to dress for success, minimize unflattering features, and maximize and highlight great features. I helped many men and women put together a wardrobe for speaking, command a room at a meeting, and create an image in sync with their brand.

➢ In summary, I showed people how to be the best versions of themselves by utilizing what they have and being ready to excel in their business, leaving a lasting impression.

Now, I've added to that problem-solving skill set how to be a purposeful and prosperous networker and live clean and toxin-free with great mental health.

Your journey to *Break Free from Your 9-to-5* may not be easy, but it will be rewarding. *Have the grit to persevere.* Get comfortable being uncomfortable. It's all about your mindset and getting out of your own way. If you don't succeed at first, have that bounce-back ability and mentality. Get back up, learn the lesson from what happened, let go of the emotion, and try again.

Don't get stopped in your tracks by imposter syndrome, either. Know you are good enough, worthy enough, and excited to do this. You are smart, experienced, confident, and ready to share your gifts with the world.

Remember: You don't have to see the whole staircase, but you do have to take the first step. In other words, all the traffic lights don't need to be green for you to go ahead and get started.

LET'S BREAK DOWN THIS 4-PART PROCESS

1) What lights you up? What brings you joy? This is the thing you are happiest doing: the thing that drives you, inspires you, lights up the inside of your soul, and that you are passionate about. This is related to your *why*.

2) What are you good at? What can you do to solve others' problems? Know what keeps people up at night. What are their pain points? The things people ask you about

all the time and you help them with might be the things you are great at. These are things you do easily that don't come easily to others. Can you identify these things?

3) Where can you or have you solved problems before? Remember the results you got for people. Where are people spending money to solve their problems for which you can also provide a solution? There are so many revenue streams available. I constantly hear about people creating opportunities, companies, and businesses.

4) What type of new business will you have? Will it start as a side hustle with the goal of becoming more and even your full-time work? Are you dedicated to replacing your JOB or just adding an additional income stream? Are you ready to *Break Free from Your 9-to-5*?

Let me expand on this.

Going from employee to entrepreneur can feel scary. It requires a shift in mindset, a willingness to take risks, and a lot of hard work. However, the reward of turning your passions into profits can be incredibly satisfying.

The first step in this process is to identify what lights you up. What are you passionate about? What skills do you possess that make you stand out from the crowd?

One of the biggest advantages of pursuing entrepreneurship is that it allows you to do work that truly makes you happy. If you're not passionate about your work, it will quickly become a burden, and you'll likely struggle to stay motivated.

Take the time to explore your passions and figure out what lights you up. This could be anything from writing to baking, from coding to gardening. Whatever it is, figure out what you enjoy and are good at.

Once you've identified your passions, figure out if there's a market for them. Can you turn your passion into a profitable business? This is an important consideration. You'll struggle to make a living if there is no demand for what you're offering.

Market research is key at this stage. Look at your competitors and see what they're doing. Are there gaps in the market you could fill? What are the trends in your industry? Conducting surveys or focus groups with potential customers can also be incredibly valuable.

Another thing to consider is whether you have the necessary skills and experience to turn your passions into a business. If not, consider taking courses or seeking mentorship or coaching from someone successful in your chosen field.

In summary, the first step in going from employee to entrepreneur and breaking free from your 9-to-5 is to figure out what lights you up. Take the time to explore your passions, think about the market demand, and assess your skills and experience. Once you clearly understand these areas, you'll be well on your way to turning your passions into profits.

IDENTIFYING YOUR STRENGTHS AND HOW TO SOLVE PROBLEMS

As you contemplate transitioning from employee to entrepreneur and breaking free for your 9-to-5, the next step is identifying your strengths and determining how to use them to solve people's problems. Here are some key steps on this journey:

- Understand your strengths and the skills you have acquired throughout your career. Take a moment to review your current or past job descriptions, your resumes, and any feedback or evaluations you've received. Identify the skills you have that are transferable and relevant to the industry you want to enter as an entrepreneur.

- After identifying your skills, think about the areas that excite you and the work you enjoy doing the most. What are your hobbies, interests, and passions? Is there a way to turn these passions into a viable business idea? This will help you identify the opportunities in the market that align with your interests and passions.
- Conduct market research to understand people's problems and identify the gaps in the industry. Think of how your skills can be used to solve these problems or fill the gaps. When you have identified the problems in the market, brainstorm ideas that could solve them. Develop a business plan that aligns with your identified passions and skills.
- It is now time to test the waters. Once you have an idea and a plan, test the waters by talking to potential customers and people in the industry. Identify if there is a demand for your product or service and whether it can be profitable. Begin by networking and getting feedback from people who are part of your target audience. This will help you refine your business plan and identify potential areas for improvement.
- Finally, take action and turn your idea into a business. Build your network, get the required training, and start marketing your business. Remember that it takes time and effort to build a successful business. Be patient and don't give up.

Going from employee to entrepreneur and breaking free from your 9-to-5 requires a mindset shift and a lot of hard work. However, you can create a roadmap to success by identifying your strengths and passions and the problems you can solve. Only take the leap when you are truly committed to your business plan and have a solid foundation of knowledge and experience from which to build.

What Will You Do?

You could take your *thing* and become an educator, advisor, consultant, coach, or mentor. Consider that one thing you do: Could you teach a workshop? Could you record, repurpose, and sell it?

I originally chose network marketing. Network marketing is a done-for-you system with low initial outlay, no overhead, and a wide array of options ranging from health and wellness to fashion, accessories, and food, to name just a few.

From my personal and professional experience and learned skill sets, I've created additional streams of income from my core network marketing company. With the age of the internet, we have a world audience at our fingertips. Mine is a global e-commerce business and a platform and vehicle to educate worldwide about toxins and their effects, as well as the correlation between the brain-gut axis and how it relates to mental health and wellness. It also offers holistic solutions and a lucrative business opportunity.

The possibilities and opportunities are endless. You could take your expertise and write a book, start a podcast, or be a guest on someone else's podcast.

Now, it's time to show the world, and of course, your sphere of influence, what you have: your original content. How will you get the word out?

Marketing is everything. Some suggestions to accomplish this are creating a course, workshop, webinar, or retreat or writing a book, speaking, networking, press releases, social media, direct mail, newsletters, email campaigns, referral partners, affiliates, or a business grand opening or ribbon cutting. You want to keep building your list; this builds your audience. Start an online group and community and create your following. Educate, inspire, and draw them to what you offer that fills their needs.

Remember what's at your *core*.

For me, it's helping men and women have options to stay at home, work from anywhere, yet be connected, to show them how to wake their sleeping giants and not be demoralized by their peers and managers in corporate, and to step out in style as the best version of themselves.

I also use the hardships I endured to connect with people that need what I offer. I was once in a very unhappy marriage. I was trying to make ends meet for 10 years after a divorce. I was in a JOB where people were negative, often taking credit for my work, while I was not being paid what I was worth.

Have you considered using your new business as a ministry or for philanthropy? How will you add value to others and make an impact on others and your community while solving their problems?

Adding value to others and impacting their community is one of the most important goals of many. It is also a way to add purpose and a mission to your business. Doing so can have a long-lasting, positive effect.

One way to effectively add value and make an impact is to focus on giving back to your community. This can come in many forms. Some people lend their skills to help build a cause they care deeply about; others volunteer their time to help those in need. A third way to give back is by donating money or goods to local charities or organizations.

No matter how you choose to give back, it helps build the community and make a positive impact.

Another way to add value to others and the community is by being a leader. People who lead by example and demonstrate qualities such as honesty, integrity, and courage are an example to others. They can inspire people to become better citizens and show them how to carry out acts of kindness, compassion, and courage that can help change the world.

Last, using our skills and talents to add value to the world is important. Utilizing our gifts and expertise to help others can have an extremely beneficial impact on our communities.

For example, someone with web design skills can volunteer to help a local business build a website. Those with medical knowledge can volunteer at a hospital or clinic. By taking the initiative to use our skills to better the lives of others, we can make a lasting, positive impact on our communities.

What About Network Marketing?

What is network marketing? Also known as multi-level marketing (MLM), network marketing is a business model that relies on a team of independent representatives to sell products or services directly to consumers. These representatives earn commissions on their sales and those of others they recruit.

If you're considering joining a network marketing company, here are some steps to get started:

1. Choose a company that aligns with your values and interests. Look for a product or service you're passionate about and believe in. This will not only make selling easier, but it will also help you build a loyal customer base.
2. Research the company and its compensation plan. Make sure you understand how you will be paid and what kind of support the company offers its representatives. Look for a company that provides training and resources to help you succeed.
3. Build your network. Contact your sphere of influence to inform them about your new venture. Attend networking events and connect with other business owners in your community. Building a successful network marketing business is all about building relationships.

4. Set goals and track your progress. Like any other business, setting goals and regularly assessing your progress is important. Use tools like a vision board or business journal to keep yourself motivated and on track.

Starting your business with a network marketing company can be rewarding and fulfilling. With dedication and hard work, you can achieve financial freedom and create the lifestyle you've always dreamed of.

So, take the first step today and begin your journey toward becoming a successful entrepreneur and breaking free from your 9-to-5.

OPTIONS THAT ARE TRENDING

Transitioning to *Break Free from Your 9-to-5* is a major step in your career path. As an entrepreneur, you are your own boss and can create your own paths.

When starting a business, it is important to consider what businesses are viable in the current market. In 2023, some of the top businesses to start include:

1. E-commerce Business
   E-commerce businesses have been a growing trend for the past few years and will continue to increase in 2023. This is because of the ease and convenience e-commerce offers to consumers. With the advancement of technology and easy access to the internet, businesses can showcase their products online and reach a larger audience. Starting an e-commerce business requires minimal capital. This makes it an accessible option for entrepreneurs. A person can start by selling a few products and expand as the market grows. With the

growth of online shopping, e-commerce has become an attractive business opportunity for entrepreneurs.

2. Online Education Business

The current global situation has impacted the education industry significantly. With the need for remote learning, online education has become increasingly popular. Starting an online education business is an ideal opportunity for those with expertise in a particular field. An individual can create and sell courses or start a tutoring business. Since everything is done online, there are no geographical limitations, making it a scalable option for entrepreneurs.

3. Mobile App Development

Mobile app development is another business opportunity that is gaining popularity. This is due to the increased use of smartphones and mobile applications. People spend significant time on their phones, making mobile apps a viable business. Entrepreneurs can create apps that cater to the specific needs of their target audience. With more businesses looking to create apps, there is a higher demand for mobile app development services.

4. Health and Wellness Business

Today, more people are concerned about their health and well-being. Starting a health and wellness business is a great idea for entrepreneurs. There are several options from which to choose, such as selling health and wellness products like supplements, creating fitness programs, or providing massage therapy services. With the increased focus on health and wellness, this business idea has a lot of potential in 2023.

5. Green Energy Business

Climate change has become a significant concern. As a result, there is an increased demand for renewable energy sources. Starting a green energy business is a great opportunity for entrepreneurs. One can consider installing solar panels or wind turbines or selling renewable energy equipment. This business has great potential as more people turn to renewable energy sources.

In summary, many ways exist to add value to others and impact our communities. Giving back, being a leader, and utilizing our skills and talents are just a few possibilities for improving the world around us. When we commit to being active participants in our communities, we can create a lasting, positive change.

You got this!

Keep going. Are you beginning to see the light at the end of the tunnel?

Are *you* ready to *Break Free from Your 9-to-5*?

8

BUDGETING TIME AND MONEY

> "**ENTREPRENEURSHIP** IS LIVING A FEW YEARS OF YOUR LIFE LIKE MOST PEOPLE WON'T, SO THAT **YOU** CAN SPEND THE REST OF **YOUR LIFE** LIKE MOST PEOPLE CAN'T."
>
> - *Adam Howell* -

TRADING TIME FOR MONEY VERSUS TRADING MONEY FOR TIME

The choice between trading time for money as an employee and trading money for time as an entrepreneur is essential to consider when deciding what career path to take. While both have advantages and disadvantages, understanding how they differ can be crucial in making the right decision for your goals.

As an employee, your time is your most valuable asset. Your job requires you to trade your time for a specified amount of money. This usually comes in the form of an hourly wage or annual salary. The amount of your pay can provide a sense of stability because it is a predictable income stream and has benefits like paid vacation, sick leave, and health insurance. However, this stability can also come at a cost. Your hours may be dictated; your job may become mundane or unfulfilling; you may feel stuck in a routine, or you might not be paid as much as you think you're worth.

On the other hand, as an entrepreneur, you can trade money for time by creating or investing in passive income streams. This allows you to have more control over your schedule and your income. Whether you own a business, invest in stocks or real estate, or license your intellectual property, each requires an initial investment of money and time to establish. However, once the systems are in place, they provide a steady, sometimes growing, revenue stream without you having to actively work for every dollar.

As an entrepreneur, you have more flexibility and freedom to choose how you use your time. However, with that freedom, expect all the risks of entrepreneurship: investments in businesses can fail, stocks can plummet, and real estate markets can crash, leaving you with less money than you initially invested.

Another advantage of being an entrepreneur is the opportunity to make more money. As an employee, your salary is limited to the pay scale set by your employer. An entrepreneur has the potential to earn limitless income through their efforts. This can be a significant motivator for individuals willing to take on the risks and responsibilities of being an entrepreneur.

As an employee, you likely received a steady paycheck and benefits. You probably had little concern for budgeting time and money beyond the standard 9-to-5 workday. However, as you embark on your journey to becoming an entrepreneur, budgeting time and money becomes crucial to your success.

Time management is an essential skill that can make or break your venture. Unlike a traditional job where your employer often delegates prioritization and deadlines, you are responsible for every aspect of your business as an entrepreneur. This means you will have to define your workday, schedule projects, and allocate time for client meetings, administrative duties, marketing, and all the other activities your business entails. Failing to budget your time effectively can lead to poor performance and loss of opportunities and ultimately hinder the growth and success of your business.

Similarly, budgeting money becomes more critical as an entrepreneur. You will likely be investing a lot of your capital and resources into your business; your finances could be at risk. Therefore, ensuring a strict budget for personal and business expenses is imperative. This includes a well-defined business plan, market research to determine the feasibility of your venture, a clear understanding of your income possibilities, and careful analysis of expenses to ensure optimal financial performance.

Budgeting time and money are critical skills for any entrepreneur. By mastering these skills, you'll be able to create an efficient, productive, and profitable business that can assist you in achieving your goals and ambitions.

For me, it was time to make a change. Actually, it was way past when I was ready to make many, many changes. How much time did I have in my day, week, and month to reevaluate how I spent my time related to my core passions and values combined with my skill set and what I was currently making a priority? You've most likely heard the analogy that you could build a luxury home in a few months by working on it full-time, or you could work on it part-time, and it will take years. The same analogy applies to building a business.

Keep going with that passion and dedication inside of you, the light at the end of the tunnel, to have your bigger purpose and calling in life come to fruition. I want to be the light in the tunnel for others to follow. Is this you, also?

I knew I wasn't ready to quit my JOB—not yet. However, I was being summoned to a higher calling.

So many people want to quit their jobs and give up their paycheck and security before it's time. This leads to anxiety and stress. A good rule of thumb is to not make the leap until you can fully live off your new business income.

So, how do you do this? How do you get there? Time to pull out your gap analysis.

Have you made a new budget? Where can you cut things out of your budget? After this, what is the minimum you need to make with your new business to walk away from your JOB?

When I had my new business alongside my JOB, I saved as much as I could from my business. How much money do you need to live on? From now on, it's important to have a budget that includes everything, including the must-haves and the things you routinely spend money on daily, weekly, and monthly. Now that you can see where your money is going, what can you eliminate or sacrifice?

The goal that's important to keep in front of you is to get to the finish line, exit your corporate job, and no longer work for anyone else. With the expenditures, you'll also want to keep track of the money coming in.

MONTHLY BUDGET

MONTH OF

INCOME			
DATE	SOURCE	CATEGORY	AMOUNT

BILLS & FIXED EXPENSES		
DATE	SOURCE	AMOUNT

VARIABLE EXPENSES		
DATE	SOURCE	AMOUNT

SUMMARY	
SOURCE	AMOUNT
INCOME	
BILLS & FIXED EXPENSES	
VARIABLE EXPENSES	
BALANCE	

BUDGETING

I began budgeting my time along with my money. The time aspect is key, so is staying focused. Make sure your family and partner, if you have one, know what your goals and timeline are. They should also know you are sacrificing short-term for long-term gain.

Every week, I found more time to work on my business as it filled my cup and brought me joy. I always had my exit from my JOB in my mind, preparing for the right time.

When first building my business, I worked for about 2 hours. That became 4, then 8, then many more. My priorities shifted as the fire burned inside me, fueling my work ethic to transition.

As I got my side hustle going, I gained confidence. I adopted a dedication to become successful and shorten my time to the finish line. I began to see nooks and crannies in my daily schedule; working on my business became more important, lucrative, and fulfilling.

Although my tech job was very busy, I got bathroom breaks and usually a lunch break. I'll never forget how I could answer a few messages while in the bathroom; my meeting-free lunches were booked with networking, follow-up, and sometimes personal development. I became very good at time management. At the end of the day, I got into the habit of making my "6 Most Important List" for the next day.

I'm all about lists. I had lists for my personal life, which included my family and kids; I had a list for business. Both lists were prioritized. I use a color-coded calendar, which I highly recommend. My lists are on my phone and mobile devices; I also have a hard copy. My calendar is broken down by day. The hours are color-coded for family and/or business, appointments for family, spiritual, IPAs, business events, and, of course, fun!

102

Daily Planner

Note: M   T   W   T   F   S   S

Schedule		Legend	
03.00		Green: **Work related activities**	
04.00			
05.00		Blue: **Personal errands /appointments**	
06.00			
07.00		Orange: **Social Events**	
08.00	Workout	Purple: **Self-Care Activities**	
09.00	Work Meeting	Pink: **Family Time**	
10.00	Work Tasks	Breakfast	Lunch
11.00	Work Tasks		
12.00	Lunch with Friend		
13.00	Work Meeting		
14.00	Work Meeting	Dinner	Snack
15.00	Dr. Apt		
16.00			
17.00	Yoga Class		
18.00	Dinner w Family	Notes	
19.00	Family Time		
20.00	Family Time		
21.00	Relaxing Reading		
22.00			
23.00			
24.00			

ORGANIZATION BRINGS GREATNESS TO NEW BUSINESS OWNERS

Having a color-coded calendar like this helps you lay out your life with your business and positions your priorities in their proper place. Set reminders on your phone. I used to be habitually late to meetings and family events—not anymore. I'm a stickler for being on time or early; again, I attribute this to great time management. This can be a great stress reliever.

Create tools and systems that help your life run smoothly. A must for me is The Effing Simple CRM ™. Time management is key no matter what you are doing. It is important in all stages of your life.

Learning how to *compartmentalize* is very useful to improve time management. Have you heard of this? Juggling a full-time career, a family, your relationships, and starting a business while taking time for self-care is a task. I equate it to balancing a bunch of plates and not letting any fall and break. If you're not organized, this is your time to get organized. It will decrease your stress while increasing your productivity—not to mention, highlight your priorities.

In my situation, I added divorcing my husband and managing time and priorities with my 4 kids between the ages of 6 and 12. This was all a journey of getting sick and tired—very sick and tired—of all the toxins in my life. This included but was not limited to my relationships, my career, and dreaming of a better life and a better version of myself showing up. That fire inside of you—your burning desire for freedom and flexibility and creating your life by design—should be growing bigger and bigger and *bigger*!

Choose your corporate exit date. This will help you visualize the light at the end of the tunnel. If you have to alter it, that's okay. However, having a date creates a mindset, a neural pathway of having a sense of urgency, dedication, hunger, and grit to go over, under, around, and through to get to your exit from corporate.

In terms of budgeting money, it is important to evaluate the monetary investment needed to make the desired life change. The cost of the desired life change should be understood so necessary funds can be allocated. It is important to consider how much money can realistically be saved or earned in the necessary timeframe. Estate planning and asset division are important considerations in budgeting for a life change. Additionally, it is important to create and maintain a reasonable budget for necessary monthly expenses.

Time management is also important in making a life change. The first step is planning for necessary steps and specific tasks within a reasonable timeline. This timeline should be realistic and achievable. A timeline should allow for contingencies and act as a buffer in case of any unexpected delays. The timeline should be regularly reviewed to ensure the desired plan of action is on track.

Making a life change can be a scary but rewarding experience. A person planning a life change must have a budget and timeline to ensure success. Budgeting time and money can help ensure a life-change plan is successful.

In addition to budgeting and timeline management, lifestyle habits must also be considered when making a life change. Working toward goals and actively changing unhealthy habits can help ensure success. Eating well, exercising, and getting enough rest are important lifestyle factors that help increase chances of success when making a life change.

Finally, support from friends and family can be invaluable when making a life change. Having a network of reliable people to support and encourage a person can make a life change much easier.

Budgeting both time and money is an essential part of the life-change process. By making a budget and appropriate timeline, as well as considering lifestyle changes, a person can set himself or herself up for success. With the right support, a life change is possible and can be greatly fulfilling.

Budgeting your time is essential when transitioning from employee to entrepreneur. With the freedom and autonomy that comes with being an entrepreneur, the challenge is to use your time in the most effective and efficient manner. To ensure you have the time and energy to focus on building a successful business, you must create a budget that works for you and your new venture.

One of the first steps of budgeting your time as an entrepreneur is determining which tasks are priorities. Prioritizing gives you the ability to develop a plan that allows you to manage your time and resources effectively. You need to be able to determine which tasks are most important and which are less important or can be delegated or outsourced.

The more efficient you are, the more successful you will be as an entrepreneur. The best way to do this is to set deadlines and break larger goals into smaller chunks that can be completed in a timely fashion. You also need to budget for some flexibility so you do not become overwhelmed or burned out from too much work.

Another important aspect of budgeting your time is creating a schedule that works for you. Make sure to include time for self-care, relaxation, and fun activities. This is important for any entrepreneur. Success in your business relies on staying focused and creative. Making time for rest, relaxation, and fun ensures you have the mental energy and enthusiasm for tackling the more difficult aspects of running a business.

Finally, having a support group with access to mentors and professionals can help you stay focused and organized as an entrepreneur. Joining a business group or organization can offer you the much-needed support and resources to help navigate the transition from employee to entrepreneur.

Budgeting your time is essential to reaching success. With a clear plan, you can prioritize tasks, stay organized and efficient, build your support network, and still take time for fun and self-care. With the right budgets, everything else falls into place.

BUSINESS PLAN

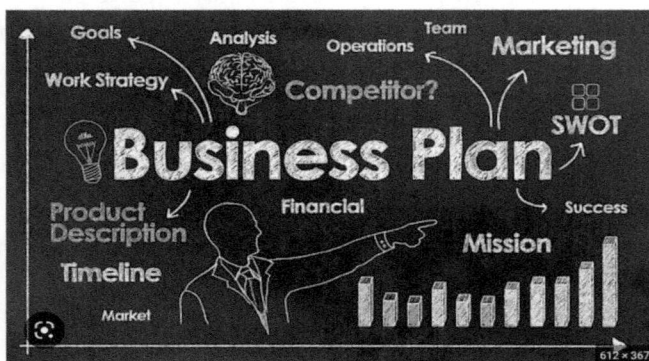

It's time to create your business plan.

If you're planning to start a business, one of the key things you should do is create a business plan. A business plan is a written document that describes your business vision, goals, objectives, strategies, and financial projections for the future.

Creating a business plan may seem intimidating; however, it doesn't have to be. This chapter will include helpful tips for writing an effective business plan.

1. Start with an Executive Summary
   An executive summary is a brief overview of your business plan. It provides a snapshot of your business, including your products or services, goals, and target market. Your executive summary should be no longer than 2 pages. It should be the first section of your business plan.
2. Describe Your Business
   In the next section of your business plan, you will describe your business in more detail. This will include information about what you're selling, who you're selling to, and what sets your business apart from competitors.

3. Identify Your Target Market

   Your business plan will include an analysis of your target market. This includes information about the size of your market, the demographics of your target audience, and any trends that may impact your business.

4. Outline Your Marketing and Sales Strategies

   In this section of your business plan, you will outline your marketing and sales strategies. This includes information about how you plan to reach your target audience, what channels you'll use to promote your business, and how you'll measure the success of your marketing efforts.

5. Describe Your Management and Operations

   Your business plan will also include information about how you plan to manage and operate your business. This includes details about your management team, organizational structure, and day-to-day operations.

6. Develop Financial Projections

   Finally, your business plan will include financial projections for your business. This includes information about your start-up costs, revenues, and profits. You will also include a cash flow statement that shows how money will flow in and out of your business over time.

In summary, creating a business plan is essential to starting a business. It can help you clarify your vision, identify your target market, and create strategies for success. By following these tips, you will be well on your way to writing a compelling, effective business plan.

If you need support writing your business plan, you can get FREE resources at your local SBA or contact www.achievesystemspro.com and become a business building member (**recommended**).

9

UP LEVELING YOUR BUSINESS AND IDEAS

MY LESSONS LEARNED AND MY TOP 20 LIST OF THINGS TO DO AND OVERCOME TO UP-LEVEL

1. Don't work to minimums; you'll always be average.
2. Set your bar of excellence high.
3. Every month, beat your best, even if only by a little bit.
4. Work to be at the top of your game, field, and company.
5. Define what success is for you, and make it happen.

6. Have an attitude of gratitude for everything you have and get done each day.
7. Count all your blessings; each is a gift.
8. Have a coach, mentor, cheerleader, and accountability partner.
9. Give back to others; it will come back to you tenfold.
10. Enthusiasm is the *electricity of life.* Light up the room or meeting you are in and illuminate others.
11. Everything happens for a reason. Embrace those signs and seize your opportunities; they can be your stepping stones to greatness.
12. Believe in yourself and be a role model for others.
13. Make a difference every day for others, adding great value to what you offer.
14. Don't keep your experience and knowledge to yourself. Share and help others make this world a better place.
15. Share your dreams, goals, and plans with everyone; they will manifest before you.
16. Have the courage and faith to pursue your dreams.
17. Surround yourself with others with similar passions, visions, and dreams.
18. Connect with others and be giving without expecting anything in return.
19. Never stop looking at the beauty around you.
20. You are only as good as your network. Weave a strong one.

I can strongly attest to the fact that my business success has been the result of several key elements:

- Awareness
- Learning key skills in verbal and nonverbal communication
- Having an image that represents my brand and me
- Networking

You've got this! Let's shape your mission and purpose.

My mission and purpose are to help people reconnect with their core values and transition out of corporate and detox, design and live their dream life with a vision that pulls them toward their greatness with confidence on the inside and style on the outside, and provide them with resources to grow sustainable businesses.

I will help you through this process as you continue to read this book.

Which one do you want to be?

Employee Vs Entrepreneur Mindset

Dream their plans	Plan their Dreams
Money is Everything	Time is Everything
Work Hard	Work Smart
Dream about Freedom	Enjoy Freedom
Trade Time for Money	Create Value for Money
Focus on $,Position	Focus on $,Significance

MINDSET SHIFT: UNLEARNING EMPLOYEE MENTALITIES AND EMBRACING AN ENTREPRENEURIAL MINDSET

Your journey from employee to entrepreneur and breaking free from your 9-to-5 is a path that requires a major shift in mindset. As an employee, you are used to taking direction from others, following established protocols, and working within specific constraints. However, an entrepreneur must embrace uncertainty, think outside the box, and take calculated risks.

To make this shift, you'll need to unlearn many of the mentalities ingrained in you as an employee. Here are some key mentalities to let go of and some new ones to adopt to embrace an entrepreneurial mindset.

EMPLOYEE MENTALITY: AVOIDING RISK

As an employee, your job is to follow specific instructions, meet deadlines, and make as few mistakes as possible. The fear of failure can be crippling; there is no incentive to take risks or try new things. This risk aversion mentality can carry over into entrepreneurship, where taking risks is often essential for growth and success.

ENTREPRENEURIAL MINDSET: CALCULATED RISK-TAKING

To succeed as an entrepreneur, you must be willing to take calculated risks. This means carefully weighing any decision's potential benefits and drawbacks and being willing to accept failure as a necessary part of the learning process. Entrepreneurs understand their success is not determined by avoiding failure but by learning from it and using it to make better decisions in the future.

EMPLOYEE MENTALITY: RIGID STRUCTURE

Working as an employee often requires following a strict set of rules and regulations. This can create a mindset of inflexibility, resulting in you being more concerned with following established protocols than finding new and innovative solutions.

ENTREPRENEURIAL MINDSET: CREATIVE PROBLEM-SOLVING

Entrepreneurs must be willing to think creatively and find innovative solutions to problems. This means being flexible and open-minded, constantly looking for new ways to approach challenges. Adapting quickly to changing circumstances and thinking outside the box is essential for success as an entrepreneur.

EMPLOYEE MENTALITY: WAITING FOR DIRECTION

As an employee, you are used to being told what to do and when to do it. You may not have a lot of autonomy or control over your work and may feel stuck in a rut.

ENTREPRENEURIAL MINDSET: SELF-DIRECTED ACTION

Entrepreneurs must be self-motivated and take charge of their success. You must be willing to set goals, create plans, and take action to make things happen. This requires a high degree of self-awareness and the ability to reflect on your actions and behavior. As a successful leader and mentor, it is important to constantly evaluate your performance and seek feedback from others to improve and better serve those who rely on you. Whether it is through responding to inquiries, offering guidance, or providing solutions to problems, your goal is to make people's lives easier and more enjoyable.

Where do you currently see your mindset in the explanations I offered above?

_____
_____
_____
_____

Changing your mindset is essential to create the success you desire in your business and life.

EVOLVE

10

THE POWER OF YOUR PROFESSIONAL PRESENCE

Life isn't about FINDING YOURSELF; It's About CREATING Yourself

LET'S BUILD YOUR GREATNESS

You did it! You have arrived. You have evolved on the inside—transformed from being an employee to being your own boss. It is now time to assess the outside.

You feel invigorated and ready to slay in your new business. Let's talk about a new image and colors that match your brand

and messaging that leaves a lasting first impression. Even if it's an online business, if you are the face of your new business, you want to be put together. You are now your personal billboard.

Fashion, image, and being put together are a big part of my success. My dress-for-success attitude propelled my corporate journey, getting me promotions and opportunities. I dressed for the position I aspired to obtain. The same applies to you as an entrepreneur. Having an image that stands out while showcasing your unique personality and style and being in sync with your new brand and business is even more important.

Know your best colors and how to dress for your body type, career, lifestyle, personality, and age. Makeup for women and hair for men and women should be flattering and neat. Have a basic and extended wardrobe in addition to your collection of accessories.

My life experiences have come full circle from being a dancer, model, engineer, leader, manager, author, speaker, makeup artist, image consultant, mom, wife, and *Glamma*. I empower others to radiate and present their inner beauty and handsomeness on the outside by embracing and harnessing their inner self and radiating it outward—so they can attract and enlighten those they want to serve.

What do these 3 words mean to you: fashion, style, image?

_____

_____

Creating your personal and professional image without sacrificing your personality and comfort is important.

We radiate our personalities with our fashions, styles, and even grooming. This is why my work includes helping top off your look with great hair, skin, and wellness.

When we love ourselves, we can then love others. We can enlighten others and become unstoppable with confidence, self-esteem, and self-love.

YOUR PERSONALITY

Your personality is where it all starts. You need to be comfortable in your skin, with who you are, and with your core values, beliefs, and personality type.

What is your personality style?

_____

_____

Do you like blending in or standing out?

_____

_____

Do you prefer conservative or trendy?

_____

_____

Do you like a loud or soft presence? (Your color volume dictates this.)

_____

_____

Do you prefer solids or prints? Are you wild about animal prints?

_____

_____

Then, there is your verbal and non-verbal communication.

While the message is important, everything about your voice, gestures, grammar, movements, mannerisms, clothes, and style will add to your impression on your audience.

Ageless Style Considerations
Fit
Style
Coloring
Body Type
Personality
Your Brand
Clothing
Makeup
To Dye or Not to Dye

How do you define ageless style? To me, it's a wardrobe, accessories, and makeup that is classic, buildable, and flattering to your age, personality, and body type. And, of course, it includes pieces and choices you are comfortable in.

_____

_____

Cherish your style. Be creative in your expression of who you are. You've come a long way. Your style reflects all things *you*.

I love the following quote by Coco Chanel:

> # BEAUTY BEGINS THE MOMENT YOU DECIDE TO BE YOURSELF
>
> COCO CHANEL

YOUR BODY TYPE

It's all about moving the shapes and colors around to minimize liabilities and maximize your assets. In other words, accentuate the curves you want and hide the others. The goal is to draw the eye down and achieve a long, lean look.

Did you know that the lower the V of your blouse/shirt, the smaller your shoulders look? It is all about illusions.

BODY TYPES

There are 7 basic body types for women and 6 for men. Know your body type and what style of pieces you need for your wardrobe to achieve your best personal style.

An example is the tough apple shape of women: round in the torso and smaller legs and arms. For this body type, you want to have an illusion of a waist by choosing pieces with a set-in waist. Or you can add a belt and have tucks at the waist to create an hourglass illusion.

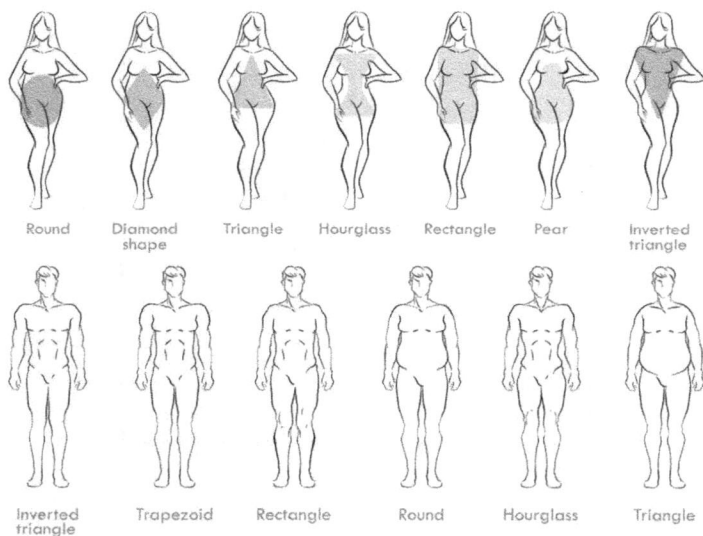

Image Courtesy Of Vexteezy

COLOR

For makeup, your skin tone plus eye color plus hair color equals your contrast level.

When we explore our physical characteristics, many of us may not consider the contrast between our hair, skin tone, and eye color. However, the combination of these features can significantly impact our overall appearance. Therefore, understanding the level of contrast between our hair, skin, and eye color can be important in defining and highlighting our style.

We must start by considering the contrast between our hair and our skin. Generally, those who have lighter skin tones have a higher degree of contrast between their hair and skin. By comparison, the contrast between those with darker skin and their hair is usually not as outwardly visible. Similarly, the contrast between our eye color and hair and skin can vary significantly. For example, those with light eyes—such as blue, hazel, or green—may have a starker contrast with their hair and skin than those with darker eyes, such as brown.

Now, let's explore how the level of contrast between these features can affect our style and overall appearance. Depending on our individual preferences, we can use the contrast between our hair, skin, and eye color to our advantage. For those who prefer a subtle look, those with high contrast between the 3 features may opt for lighter tones for their clothes and makeup to tone down the overall impact. Alternatively, those with lower contrast may emphasize the contrast provided by their features to help create a more vibrant, stunning look.

In addition, the level of contrast between our hair, skin, and eye color can also impact our perceived attractiveness. For example, in some cultures, having paler skin and darker hair and eyes is seen as more attractive. Likewise, those with higher contrast between their features—such as lighter eyes and darker hair and skin—are often viewed as more exotic and beautiful.

The level of contrast between our hair, skin, and eye color can significantly impact how we look. By understanding the contrast between our features, we can use this contrast to enhance and define our unique style and beauty. Ultimately, the level of contrast between our features is an individual choice that can help us express ourselves in a powerful, authentic way.

Light colors highlight (brighten). Dark colors minimize. The wrong shades wash out and drain you of color. The result is you look older. Most people look great in jewel tones.

Based on the contrast level of hair, eyes, and skin, some people don't look good in pastels; they look washed out.

> *The best color
> in the whole world,
> is the one that
> looks good,
> **on you.***
>
> COCO CHANEL

Light and pastel colors around the face lighten and soften.

Do you have brand colors you need to incorporate into your wardrobe?

If you haven't had a color analysis (swatch test) done, I highly recommend it. When shopping for new pieces or putting together outfits, my rule of thumb is to hold a color of clothing up to your face. If you appear to be washed out or sullen, that color is not for you. Teal is a universal color; when in doubt, wear teal.

Let's say you have a favorite color, but against your face, it doesn't look good. Use it as an accent color for your accessories or for your skirt or pants.

Step one: What is your personality? My personality is powerful, bold, and sometimes edgy. I like animal prints. What is your personality? Do you like blending into the woodwork or standing out? The rules of style have changed over the years.

A great tip when dressing for a job is to dress for the job you want.

In my previous engineering career, I dressed professionally. I was always ready to be put in front of a customer or run a meeting. It worked. I got 7 promotions in my first 14 years. Let me clarify that old cliché: "You only get one chance to make a lasting first impression." It takes 8 times to undo a bad first impression.

If you are in business, do your style and colors match your brand? Most importantly, do your colors flow with your messaging?

Beauty and good looks are skin deep—confidence is not. Do you feel better and have more confidence in an outfit you love? Your energy changes if you feel frumpy. You are unstoppable when you feel good on the inside with a positive mindset that radiates to the outside.

DRESSING FOR SPEAKING

- ✔ Know your audience.
- ✔ Be consistent with your brand and messaging.
- ✔ Show up put together. Look professional and trustworthy so you can command the room/meeting where you are speaking.
- ✔ Your presence is the mark you leave, owning your space while standing out and getting your message across.

VERBAL AND NONVERBAL COMMUNICATION

Did you realize that everything about your style sends out signals to others? It's that first impression again. When people meet or see you, they look at your clothing, expression, choice of colors, and energy while summing you up. Fashion is not only a way of showing our uniqueness but also a way of revealing our inner selves.

Throughout history, we have used fashion to differentiate ourselves, stating our uniqueness, social class, gender, and even our age group. At any given time, we may be sending non-verbal cues from our clothing, style, expressions, body language, and energy level. Or we may consciously manipulate fashion to send clear, conscious messages, such as a stern, pinstriped pantsuit paired with a lacy shell underneath that unequivocally states the wearer is all business on the outside and all woman on the inside.

Everything about our style is subject to be processed and interpreted by society, including the cut, fabric, and colors of our clothes, makeup, accessories, and hairstyle.

Nothing about interpreting fashion is exact. However, some messages are universal and easy to read. For example:

- A turtleneck top: unapproachable, aloof
- A V-neck top: open to possibilities, approachable
- A button-to-the-top jacket or shirt: closed-minded, stringent
- Big prints, metallics, or fluorescent colors: need for attention, showiness
- Miniskirt: youthfulness
- Leather, cashmere, supple suedes: wealth, decadence

Most of us quickly pick up on the non-verbal cues clothing colors send out.

- ➢ White: purity
- ➢ Black: sophistication
- ➢ Blue: loyalty
- ➢ Red: passion

Certain colors can even evoke reactions in us:

- ➢ Yellow: happiness
- ➢ Blue: calm

Style Tips for Looking Slimmer

Slimming effects for any body type are all about *balancing* your proportions.

Sometimes, it takes just a little change in how we wear things to look instantly thinner. Small changes can make a *huge* difference. All body types are going for the long, lean look.

Women's Fashion

Women have it made. Shape-wear, the right bra, dressing in monochromatic colors head to toe, color blocks vs. one color, bigger on the bottom and darker if splitting shades, constructed pieces vs. loose knits, pants that hang straight down from the hips, tailored shirts, shaped jackets, and nothing tight are all increasing in popularity.

Other great elongating styles include the sheath dress, long tunics with leggings, slim pants with a tunic, a scarf around your neck, and long necklaces. V necks add visual height and elongate the neck.

Always remember that dark colors should be minimized, and light ones should be highlighted. Wear the darkest on your heaviest part to camouflage it. Wear the lighter on your slimmer best features to highlight.

Women, if you can wear heels, the taller you look, the slimmer you look. The back pockets on your pants break up the area, making it look smaller.

For jewelry, bigger pieces next to your face, earrings, and long, layered chain necklaces give a longer, lengthening line.

For prints, if you are larger framed, big florals, thick horizontal lines, and big polka dots will make you look larger; little floral prints and pinstripes are slimming.

Makeup is amazing for a double or thick chin. Choose a darker shade than your foundation and brush upward under the chin to give a receding look. A great bronzer is good on cheekbones and temples alongside the temples.

For makeup, determine what the best products are for your age. It starts with a great, consistent skincare regimen, then colors that enhance your natural features, making your eyes sparkle.

MEN'S FASHION

The fashion world never stops changing and evolving; men's fashion trends are no different. What was once considered off-trend can become fashionable with a simple adaptation. What's trending right now may soon be passé. A constant cycle of ever-changing concepts, colors, and fabrics leaves the fashion industry buzzing. However, male fashion enthusiasts need not worry; the future of men's fashion trends looks more exciting than ever.

One of the biggest trends in men's fashion today is a return to classy, sophisticated styles from past eras. Retro-inspired looks, such as the classic pinstriped suit, have been popular for years. It seems they will stay a success in the future. Men can pair one of these suits with a classic necktie for a timeless, preppy look or break it up with a t-shirt and sneakers for a more casual aesthetic.

Another trend in men's fashion right now is athleisure. This style pulls inspiration from the sports and fitness culture, combining comfort wear with high fashion. Hoodies, tracksuits, bomber jackets, and jogger pants are some of the biggest trends in athleisure. They can be dressed up and down with sneakers, formal shoes, or even dress boots.

Regarding color and texture, neutrals are particularly popular right now. Gray, light blues, browns, and lighter shades of black are trending. These tones give off a modern, sophisticated vibe. Textured fabrics—particularly corduroy and suede—are also becoming more popular and can give an outfit a unique, eye-catching finish.

Men's fashion trends are more diverse than ever before, allowing male fashion lovers to express their styles. Retro looks, athleisure, neutrals, and textures are all on-trend and offer endless opportunities for innovators and fashion-forward shoppers. As the fashion industry keeps bouncing back with new looks, men should feel confident in their style choices, no matter the era.

Looking Younger

Mistakes to Avoid

- ✔ Just as you want to choose pieces that make you look slimmer, you may want to choose pieces that *don't* make you look older.
- ✔ Denim is youthful; tweed has the opposite effect.
- ✔ Reading glasses at the end of your nose or on your chin are a trend of the older; opt for fun, bling, tortoiseshell, or patterned glasses.
- ✔ Some can rock grey hair and look great. If you want to look younger as you age, go for warmer colors, ones flattering to your skin tone.

- ✔ Cardigans are great if slimmer, but they are unflattering and unstructured if heavier. A better choice is a constructed blazer or jacket.
- ✔ Gone are the days of frumpy shoes with so many cute, low styles out there.
- ✔ As a handbag expert, I can tell you that handbags continue to be a driving force in fashion, changing an outfit, adding a pop of color, and, of course, carrying your essentials.

The world is now your showcase. You only get one chance to make a lasting first impression. You are your billboard. Does your presence powerfully project the message you want to convey?

1. Dress for success. Your appearance can greatly affect the way people perceive and remember you. Dressing professionally and appropriately for the occasion will show that you take yourself and your work seriously.
2. Be confident. Confidence is highly attractive and communicates to others that you are knowledgeable and competent. Make sure to stand up straight, make eye contact, and speak clearly when meeting new people.
3. Listen attentively. When meeting someone for the first time, actively listen to what they have to say. This shows you respect and value their perspective and helps you learn more about them and their interests.
4. Show interest. Ask questions and show genuine interest in what the other person says. This will help establish a rapport and create a positive first impression.
5. Follow up. After meeting someone, make sure to follow up with them promptly. This can be via email or a phone call, thanking them for their time and possibly suggesting a continued conversation or meeting.

First impressions are crucial in the business world. They often determine the direction and outcome of future relationships. By being mindful of your appearance, confidence, listening skills, interest, and follow-up, you can make a lasting, positive first impression as you navigate the journey from employee to entrepreneur.

In summary, embrace who you are and love what you have. Empower yourself to make small changes for big differences in your image. Engage in and have a personal stylist; learn how to look your best. Evolve into your highest best *you* with confidence and a personal sense of style; you will be unstoppable. Enlighten others as you radiate your inner beauty and gifts outward and make a difference to those around you.

11

MASTERING FOCUS AND DISCIPLINE

T he phrase, "Your focus determines your reality," is a powerful statement. It encapsulates the essence of what you do in your life. It is a statement that speaks to the power of your thoughts and how they shape your life. In essence, what you focus on, you attract into your life.

The concept of focus is essential in determining your reality. What you focus on determines your attitude, decisions, and actions. Your focus determines what you think about, what you believe in, and what you feel. The more you focus on something, the more you believe it to be true, and the more it manifests in your reality.

To understand the power of focus, you need to understand the role it plays in your life. Your focus is like a filter that determines what you see and how you see it. It is the lens through which you view the world around you. You cannot change the world around you, but you can change how you view it. By shifting your focus, you can change your perception of reality.

When you focus on something, you activate your brain's reticular activating system (RAS). The RAS is responsible for filtering information in your brain. This helps you focus on what is important. When you focus on something, you send a message to your brain that it is important. This tells your brain that you should pay attention to it. Your brain then filters out all the irrelevant information, leaving you with a clear, focused view of what you want to achieve.

Your focus is like a magnet; it attracts what you want into your life. When you focus on something, you activate the law of attraction. This works to bring it into your life. The law of attraction states that like attracts like. So, if you focus on positive things, you attract positive things into your life. Conversely, if you focus on negative things, you attract negative things into your life.

The universe runs on the law of attraction. What you focus on grows. We all need to get to the upper vibrations and frequency of what we want, who we want to be, and where we want to be.

The power of your focus lies in its ability to shape your life. Focusing on what you want makes you more likely to achieve it. The more you focus on something, the more it becomes a part of your reality. However, focusing on what you don't want makes you more likely to attract it into your life. This is why it is essential to focus on what you want rather than what you don't want.

Successful business owners have laser focus.

Laser focus is like a horse with blinders; the horse can only focus on what is in front of it. As an entrepreneur, you must focus on what's ahead of you. Take the lessons you've learned from the past to enhance your future. Use those lessons you've learned and your experiences to shape what's ahead.

WHAT ARE YOU FOCUSING ON?

What would you do if you could be, do, or have anything you desire and knew you couldn't fail?

Will you waste your time thinking about what's not right and what you don't like? Or are you ready to focus on what you want, what you deserve, and what you were put on this earth to do—your soul's purpose?

> ➤ Flow your thoughts and energy.
> ➤ Organize your dreams, goals, and desires.
> ➤ Make a conscious effort.
> ➤ Have unwavering dedication.
> ➤ Set your intentions.

In today's ever-competitive world, transitioning out of corporate and into self-employment can be a little scary but rewarding. It is important to focus on the goals and objectives that can be achieved and the effort required to make the transition successful. With laser focus and dedication, the transition from corporate to self-employment and breaking free from your 9-to-5 can be made much easier.

You are already on your way to *Break Free from Your 9-to-5*. You've assessed your goals, ambitions, and desired lifestyle. A critical element of success is a deep understanding of what you are working toward and what success looks like. It is also important to consider the type of work you enjoy and the path you need to take to achieve these goals. A clear, achievable plan is essential to ensure your transition is successful.

Once the destination is defined, it is time to take the necessary steps to craft a strategy for success. Creating a budget and setting aside finances for investing in oneself is important. Allocating funds for acquiring a skill set, obtaining resources, and learning new technology will help differentiate oneself and gain competitive advantages. Having an effective marketing strategy is also essential. This helps you reach out to potential clients and promote your business.

Maintaining focus and dedication is vital throughout the transition process to emerging success. Highly focused entrepreneurs make the most of their time by filtering out distractions and focusing on the task at hand. Maintaining a strong social network is also important; this ensures helpful advice and guidance are always available. Establishing a network of mentors, family, friends, and colleagues can help provide moral support and unbiased feedback to help make the right decisions.

What you focus on grows. Staying focused can be challenging for anyone, regardless of age or profession. Focusing is particularly difficult in today's digital world, with so many electronic devices and distractions at our fingertips. Fortunately, there are several tips and techniques to help you stay focused and maintain good concentration.

❖ One of the best tips for staying focused is maintaining a good posture and controlling your environment. Sitting in an ergonomic office chair or using a standing desk in an area with minimal distractions can improve your concentration.

❖ Other good tips include getting enough sleep and having a healthy diet. Keeping your body and mind healthy ensures you can concentrate and stay focused when you sit down to work.

❖ In addition to a good sleep schedule and diet, maintaining a consistent schedule can be beneficial. Start each day with a plan of how you'll spend your time. Set achievable, reasonable goals, and strive to complete them. To stay focused while working, consider setting a timer to break up your tasks into manageable chunks. This will help you stay on track. It also adds a sense of accomplishment as you complete each interval and move on to the next.

❖ It's also important to control the amount of electronic distractions. We live in a world of constant notifications. Notifications pop up on our devices, making it hard to concentrate. Put away your devices, turn off the notifications, choose a specific time to check them, and stick to it.

❖ Learning to be mindful can be a helpful tool for staying focused. When you feel overwhelmed or distracted, acknowledge it and take a few minutes to breathe and clear your mind. This is a good way to stay in the *here and now* and be mindful of the task at hand.

Staying focused can be difficult. However, with a few simple tips and techniques, it is possible to stay focused and productive. Planning, limiting distractions, staying healthy, and being mindful are all methods to help improve focus. With practice, these techniques can lead to improved concentration and productivity.

DISTRACTIONS AND SELF-DISCIPLINE

As an entrepreneur, time is a valuable resource that cannot be wasted. Limiting distractions and practicing self-discipline are essential to maximize productivity and achieve success. As an entrepreneur, you must develop a laser-like focus on your goals and objectives. This requires blocking out external distractions and maintaining a high degree of self-control.

One of the biggest challenges you'll face as an entrepreneur is the constant bombardment of distractions. With emails, phone calls, social media notifications, and other distractions, staying focused on the task at hand can be difficult. However, by limiting these distractions, you can increase your productivity and efficiency. As I indicated earlier, setting aside specific times to check email or respond to phone calls can prevent constant interruptions and allow for uninterrupted work time.

To practice self-discipline, you, as an entrepreneur, must prioritize and stay committed to your goals. This means setting clear objectives and developing a plan to achieve them. It also requires being honest about what behaviors and habits limit productivity and consciously changing them. For example, if you have trouble avoiding the temptation of social media during work hours, you can set a goal to take a break only after completing a certain number of tasks.

Creating a routine and sticking to it is an effective way to maintain self-discipline. Establishing a regular schedule for work, exercise, and leisure activities can help set a routine, reduce decision fatigue, and make it easier to stay on track. By having a set routine, you can avoid wasting mental energy on deciding what to do next. Instead, you can focus your energy on executing tasks.

In addition to limiting distractions and practicing self-discipline, you must recognize that taking breaks is okay. Everyone needs time to recharge. Rest is essential in maintaining mental and physical health. Taking breaks helps restore your focus and improves overall productivity. By prioritizing breaks in your daily routines, you can ensure you work smarter, not harder.

In summary, limiting distractions and practicing self-discipline are crucial if you want to achieve success. You can increase your focus and efficiency by developing a routine, setting clear goals, and limiting distractions. This leads to better results in less time.

In a world where distractions are everywhere, it's essential to prioritize work and stay committed to achieving goals. Through self-discipline and intentional actions, you can improve your productivity, use your time better, and achieve your goals.

OUR THOUGHTS

Our lives and the directions we take are fundamentally shaped by our thoughts, for good or for ill. As the proverb says, "Your thoughts become your words; your words become your actions; your actions become your habits, and your habits become your future."

As human beings, our greatest asset is our ability to think, feel, reason, and create. Even though your environment, individual physiology, and circumstantial influences all play a role in your life, your thoughts are the power you yield to create your reality and destiny.

Therefore, mindful thoughts are paramount to achieving your goals and making positive changes. Your thoughts are what you take with you into your future. It is important to be intentional in their creation. You must remind yourself to treat your mind with respect and appreciation, tending to them and allowing them to thrive. After all, what you think will, without fail, become your future reality.

When it comes to our thoughts, focus is everything. Much like an artist homing in on their desired masterpiece or a dancer refining their choreography, you must refine your thoughts to create the life you seek. You must be mindful of what you are permitting your mind to hold. You must understand that your focus and intentions shape the structures that exist in your life today and in your future. This can mean tuning into the aspects of your life you wish to see flourish or steering clear of those aspects you find unhealthy and unproductive.

To make sure your highest thoughts are being heard and given the utmost priority, you should commit to consistency and reflection. This can involve setting aside intentional time to practice quieting the noise within your mind and connecting with your truest, highest self. Allowing this space and these moments helps prevent your thoughts from wandering unchecked. Instead, allowing this space and these moments keeps your thoughts focused on your desired destiny.

Ultimately, it is up to you to shape your future and create the life of your dreams. Our thoughts are powerful. Positive thinking can amplify joy and well-being; negative thinking can do the opposite. Living your best life starts with cultivating thoughts that serve you and guide you toward your desired goals and away from undesirable paths. Our thoughts become our words; our words become our actions; our actions become habits, and our habits become our destinies.

What exactly does success mean to you? Knowing this will help you find joy and fulfillment in your journey. Success has many definitions. However, when transitioning from employee to entrepreneur and breaking free from your 9-to-5, success means more than financial stability and freedom. It's also about having dreams, taking risks, and finding fulfillment in what you do in life.

Success as an entrepreneur means having an appreciation for your journey. Before you can experience financial rewards, you must invest a lot of time, effort, and soul-searching into your business idea. It requires you to take a leap of faith more than anything else. It takes courage, a willingness to dive into the unknown, and the understanding that failure is just as much a part of success as winning. As an entrepreneur, you need to be okay with the challenge of creating something from scratch and comfortable with uncertainty.

Success also means taking risks and remaining committed to your goals, even in the face of adversity. As an entrepreneur, failure isn't an option. It's essential to take the time to plan and execute and remain focused no matter what distractions come your way to create a successful business. Success for an entrepreneur means having the discipline and resilience to stick with your vision and learn from your mistakes.

Success isn't just about making money; it's about making an impact in other people's lives. Do you love doing that? Is being a difference-maker important to you?

As an entrepreneur, success means finding satisfaction in helping others. Knowing you're making a difference in the lives of your customers, clients, or employees can be a great source of joy and fulfillment. Whether through providing a valuable service, creating jobs, or simply inspiring others, you can achieve success as an entrepreneur by contributing to society.

To successfully transition from employee to entrepreneur, you must have a clear vision, an unwavering commitment, and a desire to add value to the world. Making the leap takes courage; those driven by the right reasons find success sweet and rewarding.

The journey from corporate to self-employment can be scary and challenging. With the right laser focus, it can also be rewarding and fulfilling. By assessing your goals, crafting a plan, and dedicating yourself to meeting these objectives, the transition from corporate to self-employment can be a success. However, knowing exactly what success means to you is essential to your fulfillment.

THE POWER OF MEDITATION

Meditation is an ancient practice that has been passed down through generations for thousands of years. It is a method for achieving clarity, calmness, and peace of mind. Meditation can be considered as a tool for personal transformation and growth. In recent years, the practice of meditation has gained immense popularity due to its beneficial effects on mental and physical health.

Many people have used meditation as a tool to transform their lives, especially when considering a major life change like transitioning from employee to entrepreneur and breaking free from your 9-to-5. Do you practice meditation? Such a move requires you to shift your mindset, like I did, and have the right mental state and preparedness for the unknown. Meditation can greatly help you in achieving these goals.

Meditation has a reputation for being a mystical and difficult practice that requires extensive experience to master.

Fortunately, it is actually a simple technique that requires only a few minutes to be effective. Anyone can learn meditation regardless of age, sex, or spiritual beliefs.

The power of meditation can clear your mind and bring focus and clarity to your thoughts. It will allow you to disconnect from the outside world's noise and connect with your inner self. Meditation helps reduce anxiety, stress, and depression. It has been shown to improve cognitive functions such as memory, attention, and perception. Most importantly, it promotes a positive, calm mind state that makes it easier to navigate life changes productively.

MEDITATION AND ENTREPRENEURSHIP

Entrepreneurship is a challenging yet rewarding experience. It requires a level of skill, creativity, and persistence not often found in traditional careers. It also requires a mindset focused on success and motivation, which can be stressful.

Meditation can help mitigate these stressors by providing a sense of calm and clarity of mind. It also helps you, as an entrepreneur, *Break Free from Your 9-to-5* and become more focused and present. This is crucial for your productivity and creativity. Meditation can provide the mental state you need as an entrepreneur to succeed.

The following are some of the ways meditation can be helpful when transitioning from employee to entrepreneur and breaking free from your 9-to-5:

✔ Meditation helps develop the ability to focus on the present moment rather than becoming distracted by external stimuli, such as social media notifications, emails, or phone calls. This ability to focus can be particularly helpful when transitioning from employee to entrepreneur and breaking free from your 9-to-5.

As an entrepreneur, it is important to be present and focused on what needs to be done rather than becoming distracted by peripheral information.

✔ Meditation also helps you develop focus and concentration. As an entrepreneur, you will have to multitask and prioritize your goals. You must focus on what is most important at any given time. Meditation helps you train your mind to be present and fully engaged in the moment. It also helps you let go of distractions and achieve the clarity necessary to make better decisions. When you are fully focused, you are more likely to be productive and efficient. This can lead to a greater chance of success as an entrepreneur.

✔ Meditation helps you manage stress and anxiety. Starting a business can be overwhelming; stress is inevitable. It is important to develop techniques that can help you manage the stress and anxiety that come with the territory of entrepreneurship. When you meditate, your body and mind enter a state of relaxation. This can help reduce stress and anxiety. By incorporating meditation into your routine, you can learn to manage the demands of starting and growing a business more healthily.

✔ Meditation can help you develop a growth mindset. In entrepreneurship, you need to have an open mind to learn from the feedback from other entrepreneurs, mentors, and clients. Meditation helps you create this mind space. When you practice meditation, your mind becomes more open and receptive. This means you are more likely to embrace challenges and see them as opportunities for growth rather than threats. By adopting a growth mindset, you are more likely to be resilient in the face of adversity and better able to bounce back from setbacks.

✔ Meditation helps you tap into your intuition. As an entrepreneur, you will need to make tough decisions, preferably based on your intuition. As you meditate and tap into your intuition, you become more self-aware because meditation activates your subconscious mind. This can help you make decisions on data vs. intuition, which has the potential to swallow a business whole.

GETTING STARTED

If you're interested in getting started with meditation, there are a few key steps you can take to ensure you start on the right foot.

First, it's important to set aside time for meditation each day. The exact amount of time you set aside is up to you. It's generally recommended to start with just a few minutes and work your way up as you become more comfortable with the practice. Setting aside the same time each day can help you establish a routine and make incorporating meditation into your daily life easier.

Next, you'll want to find a quiet, comfortable place to meditate. This could be a corner of your bedroom, a peaceful outdoor area, or any other location where you feel calm and relaxed. You may also consider using props, such as a cushion or blanket, to make yourself more comfortable during meditation.

Once you're ready to begin meditating, there are a variety of techniques you can try. One popular method is mindfulness meditation. This involves simply focusing on your breath and observing your thoughts without judgment. Other techniques might focus on visualization, mantras, or body scans.

Regardless of your chosen technique, it's important to remember that meditation is a practice. You may not see immediate results. It's important to be patient and trust the process.

In addition to these practical steps, it's also important to cultivate a mindset of openness and curiosity concerning meditation. Don't be afraid to experiment with different techniques. Seek guidance from those either experienced in meditation or teachers of meditation. Everyone's meditation journey is different; what works for one person may not work for another.

Getting started with meditation is all about finding what works for you and committing to a regular practice. With dedication and patience, you can reap the many benefits of meditation, including increased focus, reduced stress, and a greater sense of overall well-being.

Maintaining Work-Life Balance: Avoiding Burnout and Prioritizing Self-Care as an Entrepreneur

The journey from employee to entrepreneur and breaking free from your 9-to-5 comes with its share of difficulties and challenges. While the freedom, creativity, and control that come with being an entrepreneur may seem highly desirable, there's a possibility that the workload and business demands could lead to burnout. Entrepreneurs often put in long hours, work on their businesses during the weekends and holidays, and struggle to balance work and life. So far in this chapter, we have been exploring tips, strategies, and techniques to help maintain work-life balance, avoid burnout, and prioritize self-care.

Why is Work-Life Balance Important for Entrepreneurs?

Work-life balance, also known as work-life integration, is the act of balancing your work life with your personal life.

Achieving work-life balance provides many benefits to you as an entrepreneur. These benefits include:

- Improved mental health and well-being: By balancing your work and personal life, you can reduce the likelihood of suffering from depression, anxiety, or stress.
- Increased productivity: A balanced work-life will help you avoid burnout and increase motivation, resulting in improved productivity.
- Stronger personal relationships: By prioritizing and spending more time with family and friends, you can improve your personal relationships, which translates to a happier life.
- Creativity: Engaging in various fun activities can help you find inspiration and creativity, leading to increased innovation in your work.

STRATEGIES FOR MAINTAINING WORK-LIFE BALANCE AS AN ENTREPRENEUR

1. Set boundaries. One of the key elements of work-life balance as an entrepreneur is setting boundaries. Entrepreneurs commonly find themselves responding to emails late into the night, missing family events, or scheduling meetings during their free time. If not corrected, such habits could decrease productivity and diminish health. Entrepreneurs can set boundaries between their work and personal lives to prevent this. For example, consider setting a time when you stop checking work emails or scheduling meetings. Let your clients or customers know you operate within your specific working hours and prevent work from spilling into your personal life.

2. Prioritize quality time with family and friends. It's vital to allocate quality time to friends and family. Often, entrepreneurs spend long hours working in their businesses and losing touch with family members and friends. Keep your business communications separate. Make a clear distinction between your work life and your personal life. By keeping your business communication separate, you can maintain a professional image and avoid potential misunderstandings that can arise when mixing work and personal matters.

One way to keep your business communication separate is to have a separate email address or phone number for work-related messages and calls. This allows you to easily differentiate between messages requiring your attention during work hours and those that can wait.

Another option is to create separate social media accounts or profiles for professional purposes. This helps you maintain a professional image online and avoid potential conflicts between your personal and professional interests.

Finally, it's important to establish clear boundaries when it comes to communicating with colleagues or clients outside of work hours. Make it clear when you are available and when you are not. Try to avoid the temptation to check work-related messages during your personal time.

By keeping your business communication separate and establishing clear boundaries, you can improve your work-life balance and maintain a healthy level of productivity and focus.

Last, let's talk about self-discipline.

PHYLLIS MARLENE BENSTEIN

THE POWER OF SELF-DISCIPLINE IN BECOMING A SUCCESSFUL ENTREPRENEUR

The journey from employee to entrepreneur and breaking free from your 9-to-5 requires a lot of self-discipline. Self-discipline is controlling your behavior and taking responsibility for your actions. It means doing what you need to do even when you don't feel like it. Self-discipline is not only important in your personal life, but it is also critical in your entrepreneurial journey.

Entrepreneurship requires a lot of hard work and dedication; self-discipline is the key to achieving success. Without self-discipline, getting distracted and losing focus on your goals is easy. This leads to procrastination and missed opportunities.

Here are some reasons self-discipline is so important on your journey from employee to entrepreneur and breaking free from your 9-to-5:

1. Helps you prioritize your goals: A self-disciplined individual knows how to prioritize their goals and focus on what is essential. As an entrepreneur, it is vital to have clarity about your goals. Self-discipline helps you stay on track and take action toward achieving them.
2. Ensures consistency: Consistency is the key to success in entrepreneurship. Self-discipline helps you stay consistent in your efforts. This is necessary for building a successful business. Without consistency, your business will not thrive.
3. Builds resilience: Self-discipline builds resilience and helps you push through difficult times. As an entrepreneur, you will face challenges, setbacks, and failures. It is essential to have the discipline to keep going during difficult times.

4. Increases productivity: Self-discipline helps you avoid distractions and stay focused on your goals. This leads to increased productivity and efficiency, which is critical in the entrepreneurial world.

5. Improves time management: Time is a critical resource in entrepreneurship. Self-discipline helps you manage your time effectively. You can maximize your productivity and achieve your goals by prioritizing your tasks and avoiding time-wasting activities.

Becoming a successful entrepreneur requires a lot of hard work, dedication, and self-discipline. Self-discipline is the foundation for achieving success in all aspects of life and is critical in entrepreneurship. By developing self-discipline, you can prioritize your goals, stay consistent, build resilience, increase productivity, and improve your time-management skills.

Start working on your self-discipline today. You will be on your way to achieving your entrepreneurial dreams.

Summary

Throughout this chapter, we have discussed the importance of avoiding distractions and developing self-discipline to stay focused on our goals. We also touched on the role our thoughts play in our ability to maintain focus and suggested incorporating meditation into your daily routine as a means of strengthening your focus muscles.

We also emphasized the need to balance your work and personal life to avoid burnout. You were reminded to take breaks and allow for downtime, which are crucial for maintaining productivity over the long term. I encourage you to be mindful of your energy levels and prioritize self-care practices that help you recharge and focus on your goals.

Focus is a skill that can be developed and honed over time through consistent practice and self-awareness. Finding a sustainable balance in your work and personal life is essential to achieving long-term success.

12
CONTINUOUS GROWTH AND LEARNING

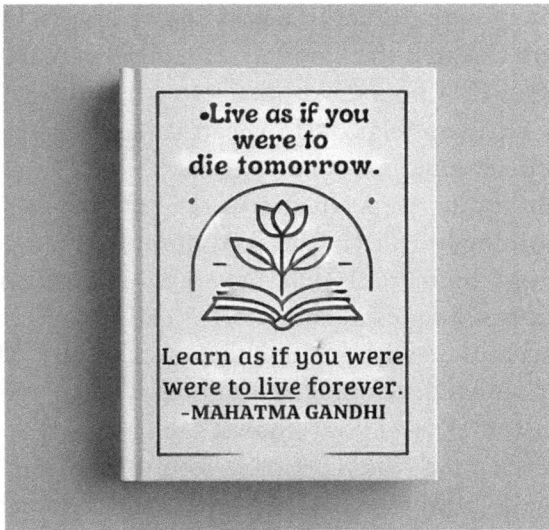

•Live as if you
were to
die tomorrow.

Learn as if you were
were to <u>live</u> forever.
-MAHATMA GANDHI

One of the most important elements of success as an entrepreneur is a commitment to continuous growth and learning. This commitment isn't just about gaining more knowledge but also about staying relevant, adaptable, and open to new ideas and opportunities. It's about cultivating a mindset that embraces lifelong learning and the belief that there is always room to expand your skills and expertise.

Continuous growth means actively seeking resources and opportunities that allow you to develop personally and professionally. One of the best ways to do this is by joining professional organizations that align with your field, industry, or entrepreneurial journey. For me, being part of groups like Achieve Systems has been transformative. Achieve Systems, a network of successful professionals dedicated to supporting business growth, offers resources, education, and a community of like-minded individuals. Whether through networking events, workshops, or peer-to-peer mentorship, I have found that surrounding myself with driven people has been a catalyst for my growth. There is always the option to build your community through the Connect & Collaborate networking event system in a box. Continual growth through building authentic business relationships can catapult your business growth and revenue.

Beyond industry-specific networks like Achieve Systems, consider joining broader business communities like your local Chamber of Commerce. Chambers provide excellent opportunities for building local connections, gaining visibility, and keeping up to date with regional business trends. Many also offer professional development programs to help you sharpen your skills and expand your knowledge base.

When selecting which organizations to join, choose those that resonate with your business goals and personal values. Look for groups that offer a mix of educational content, networking opportunities, and leadership development.

For example, professional networks, entrepreneurial mastermind groups, or industry associations can provide valuable insights and support.

Another essential aspect of continuous growth is staying current with industry trends. Subscribe to relevant newsletters, read industry publications, and follow thought leaders in your space. Podcasts, webinars, and online courses can also be invaluable resources for keeping up with your field's latest strategies, tools, and technologies. As the business landscape evolves, staying informed will allow you to anticipate changes and seize new opportunities before others recognize them.

Last, remember that growth isn't always about consuming new information; it's also about applying what you've learned and reflecting on your experiences. Take time to assess your progress regularly, identify areas for improvement, and set new learning goals. Consider seeking a coach or mentor who can provide you with a fresh perspective and guide you in achieving your next level of success.

In short, commit to never becoming stagnant. Whether it's through joining professional organizations, engaging in local business communities, or staying on top of industry advancements, embrace the journey of continuous learning. Doing so will keep you energized, inspired, and well-equipped to face the ever-changing world of entrepreneurship.

ENLIGHTEN

13

LIVING, LEADING, AND LEAVING YOUR LEGACY

> The idea is not
> *to live forever,*
> but to create
> *something*
> *that will.*
>
> —
>
> ANDY WARHOL

When most people think of legacy, they usually think of the impact they will leave behind after they pass away. While that is certainly a part of it, true legacy is so much more than that. Living your legacy means living your values and beliefs every day and integrating them into all aspects of your life, including your business.

As you make the transition from employee to entrepreneur and *Break Free from Your 9-to-5*, it is important to think about what you want your legacy to be.

> ➤ What do you want to be remembered for?
> ➤ What impact do you want to have on the world?

Although these are big questions, they are critical for building a truly meaningful and fulfilling business.

LIVING YOUR LEGACY

To live your legacy in your business, start by defining your values and mission. These are the guiding principles your business will be built around. They should be at the forefront of everything you do.

For example, if you value sustainability, you may choose to create a business focused on environmentally friendly products or services. If you value community, you may choose to work with local suppliers and hire employees from your local area.

Once you have defined your values and mission, ensuring they are integrated into every aspect of your business is important. This includes your branding, marketing, product development, and customer service. Make sure that every interaction with your business reflects your values and mission and that you stay true to them even as your business grows and evolves.

Living your legacy also means taking responsibility for your actions and being accountable to yourself and your stakeholders. This includes being transparent about your business practices, respecting your employees and customers, and giving back to your community. By doing so, you will build a strong reputation and earn the trust and loyalty of your stakeholders.

As you build your business and live your legacy, it's important to remember that it's not just about what you do but also about *how* you do it. By staying true to your values and mission and striving to make a positive impact, you can build a business that is both successful and meaningful. Ultimately, that is the legacy you will leave behind.

If you are working on living a legacy, here are some helpful questions for your consideration:

1. What do I want to be remembered for?

_____

_____

2. What impact do I want to have on the world?

_____

_____

3. What values do I want to represent?

_____

_____

4. What qualities do I want to develop and demonstrate?

_____

_____

5. What actions can I take to inspire others and make a difference?

_____

_____

6. How can I use my talents and resources to contribute to the greater good?

_____

_____

7. How can I create a meaningful and fulfilling life that aligns with my legacy goals?

_____

_____

8. Who are the people I admire, and how can I learn from their legacies?

_____

_____

9. What steps can I take to ensure my legacy endures beyond my lifetime?

_____

_____

10. How can I live each day with purpose and intention to create the legacy I desire?

_____

_____

LEADING YOUR LEGACY

As an entrepreneur, you have the unique opportunity to create a legacy that outlives you. Unlike being an employee, where your contribution is limited to your job description and immediate team, building a business allows you to impact your community, industry, and the world.

To lead your legacy, you must clearly envision what you want to achieve and how your business will positively impact others. This vision should be communicated clearly to your team, customers, and partners so they can understand the purpose of your work. In doing so, they will become advocates for your brand.

Building a sustainable business is one way to ensure your legacy lasts beyond your lifetime. That means creating systems and processes that can withstand the test of time and minimize your environmental impact. Look for ways to reduce waste, use renewable resources, and contribute to your local community.

Another important aspect of leading your legacy is investing in your team. While you may be the founder and CEO of your company, you cannot do everything alone. Building a strong team allows you to delegate tasks and responsibilities, freeing up time for you to focus on your strengths and strategic goals.

In addition to investing in your team, it's important to prioritize your development as a leader. Staying up to date with industry trends, attending conferences and workshops, and reading books can help you hone your skills and become a more effective leader. You can also seek mentors or advisors who can provide guidance and constructive feedback.

As you work toward building a lasting legacy, don't forget to celebrate your accomplishments along the way. Recognizing your team's hard work and dedication and acknowledging your business's positive impact on society can help you stay motivated and inspired.

In summary, leading your legacy means taking a long-term view of your business and making choices that benefit your bottom line, your community, and the environment. It means investing in your team and your growth as a leader, communicating your vision for your business clearly, and celebrating your successes. By doing so, you can build a legacy that will make a lasting impact on the world.

The journey from employee to entrepreneur is transformational. There is no denying that it takes a leap of faith, courage, and determination to step away from the comfort of a steady paycheck, benefits, and job security to venture into the unknown. This journey is filled with challenges, setbacks, and uncertainty. However, for resilient people committed to leaving a legacy, it can be the most rewarding and fulfilling journey of their lives.

If you are working on leading a legacy, here are some helpful questions for your journey:

1. What values and principles do I want to instill in future generations?

   _____

   _____

2. How can I make a positive impact on my community and society as a whole?

   _____

   _____

3. What skills and knowledge must I acquire to successfully lead a legacy?

   _____

   _____

4. What steps can I take to ensure my legacy is sustainable and long-lasting?

   _____

   _____

5. How can I involve and inspire others to contribute to my legacy?

   _____

   _____

6. What lessons have I learned from past leaders and their legacies?

   _____

   _____

7. How can I adapt and innovate to fulfill my legacy in an ever-changing world?

   _____

   _____

8. What resources and support do I need to achieve my legacy goals?

_____

_____

9. How can I measure the success of my legacy and make necessary adjustments?

_____

_____

10. How can I ensure my legacy is inclusive and represents diverse perspectives?

_____

_____

LEAVING YOUR LEGACY

For many, the motivation to become an entrepreneur stems from creating something meaningful, building a business that provides value to others, making a difference, and leaving a legacy. The legacy an entrepreneur leaves behind is not just about the business they build or the products they create. It goes beyond that. It is the impact they have on people's lives, the difference they make in their communities, and the mark they leave on the world.

When you, as an entrepreneur, set out to build a legacy, you are not just building a business; you are building a reputation, brand, culture, and community. You are creating something that will outlast you and continue to grow and thrive long after you are gone. You are building something that will be remembered and celebrated for generations to come.

One of the most important things you as an entrepreneur can do to leave a lasting legacy is to stay true to your values and beliefs. When you start a business or embark on a new venture, you should do it with intention, purpose, and authenticity.

You should be clear about what you stand for, what you want to achieve, and what you want the business to represent.

When entrepreneurs stay true to their values and act with integrity, they create a culture of trust, respect, and transparency. This culture attracts customers and clients and inspires employees and partners to align themselves with the company's vision and mission.

Another way you, as an entrepreneur, can leave a legacy is by giving back to your community. You can do this by supporting local charities, volunteering your time and resources, and investing in initiatives that make a positive impact. When you give back to your community, you'll create a ripple effect of positivity that benefits everyone.

Last, as an entrepreneur, you can leave a legacy by passing on your knowledge, skills, and experience to the next generation of entrepreneurs. You can mentor and guide young entrepreneurs, share your stories, and inspire others to follow in your footsteps. By doing so, you contribute to the growth and development of others, their communities, and beyond. Please ask yourself the following:

1. What legacy do I want to leave?

_____

_____

2. What values and principles do I want to be remembered for?

_____

_____

3. What impact do I want to have on society and future generations?

_____

_____

4. How can I contribute to my community or leave a positive mark on the world?

_____

_____

5. What achievements or accomplishments do I want to be remembered for?

_____

_____

6. How can I instill my knowledge, skills, and wisdom into others?

_____

_____

7. How can I create a lasting impact through philanthropy or volunteer work?

_____

_____

8. How can I inspire and motivate others to continue my legacy?

_____

_____

9. How can I ensure my legacy aligns with my personal beliefs and goals?

_____

_____

10. How can I use my experiences and lessons learned to benefit others?

_____

_____

11. What actions can I take now to start building my legacy?

_____

_____

LET'S GET STARTED

Living, leading, and leaving a legacy are all connected and require careful planning and intentional action. Here are some steps you can take to start your journey.

PHYLLIS MARLENE BENSTEIN'S LIST OF 7 IMPORTANT THINGS

1. **Define Your Values**: Identify the values most important to you and make a list. Think about what you stand for, what you want to be known for, and what motivates you.
2. **Determine Your Purpose:** Establish your sense of purpose by reflecting on what you are most passionate about and what gives you a sense of meaning or fulfillment.
3. **Craft a Vision:** Once you have identified your values and purpose, create a vision for how you want to live, lead, and leave a legacy. Think big and aim high.
4. **Set Goals:** Set specific, measurable, attainable, relevant, and time-bound goals that align with your values, purpose, and vision. Break down your goals into smaller, achievable steps.

5. **Take Action:** Act on your goals and make progress toward your vision. Stay focused on your priorities; consistently take steps forward.
6. **Make an Impact:** Share your knowledge, skills, and resources. Make a positive impact in your community, organization, or industry.
7. **Reflect and Refine.** Regularly reflect on your progress and adjust your plan as needed. Think about what you have learned and how you can continue to grow and evolve.

Insert these 7 action steps above and then lead it to implementation.

Follow the checklist in Exhibit A to organize your success strategies.

Use the reference section in Exhibit B to find more help.

14

BE A LIGHT

> "If all your prayers
> were answered,
> would it change the
> world or just yours?"
>
> @FAITH IMAGE

You've come a long way.

Your light has been enhanced and enlarged. With current world situations and environments, many people are experiencing a dimming of their lights. Philanthropy, using your business as a ministry, and giving to causes and projects in alignment with your core values and beliefs are ways to do this.

Be a light—a force of good—with your new business ventures. The idea of being a light and sharing your gifts is a concept that touches on an important aspect of human existence—the notion that our lives are enriched when we contribute something of ourselves to the world around us. As individuals, you often have unique talents, passions, and resources you can offer to others. By taking advantage of your gifts and abilities and putting them to use to benefit others, you can be a source of light for yourself and those around you.

First, you can use your gifts and talents to aid those who are less fortunate. Whether it is your physical strength, artistic capabilities, or intellectual prowess, you possess abilities that can be used to better the lives of others.

For example, you could offer to tutor a struggling student or someone struggling to learn a language or help someone who resides in a poverty-stricken area and needs essentials. By utilizing the special capabilities you have been blessed with, you can be a source of hope and assurance to those struggling around you.

Second, you can use your gifts and talents to positively influence the world beyond yourself. Whether through your writing, music, art, activism, or simple presence in the world, you can be a force of good in the lives of many. Use your gifts to lift a voice of knowledge, be a catalyst of change, and create a more just and equitable world. By tapping into your skills and resources, you can be a beacon of light to many.

Third, you can use your gifts and talents to positively contribute to the world in terms of your actions and attitude. You can be a source of light in the darkest times by spreading positivity, engaging in meaningful dialogue, taking action when necessary, and advocating for the things you believe in. By engaging in self-reflection and recognizing the potential you have to make a positive impact, you can be a force of hope and healing in this world.

By being a light and sharing your gifts with the world, you can transform your life as well as the lives of those around you. From aiding those who need it to engaging in meaningful action, you possess the power to be a source of hope and healing. You can become a beacon by recognizing your worth and leveraging the special capabilities you have been blessed with.

Metaphorically, being a light to me means lighting or enlightening someone's light that is dim or dimming. Enlightening others whose light may be dim is a noble undertaking, calling for a kind, empathetic approach. There are many ways to support and encourage those whose light appears to have dimmed. The primary focus should be providing an empathetic atmosphere where individuals can feel safe and protected. This will give them the courage to explore their feelings without fear of being judged or ridiculed.

One way to offer support and encouragement is through encouraging conversations. This can be done in a personal, one-on-one setting or in support groups. These conversations can be helpful in allowing the individual to express their feelings and gain a better understanding of their current struggles. They may also help identify potential avenues for change and personal growth.

Taking action is another way to offer support and enrichment to others whose light may be dim. This could involve providing practical support such as helping with daily tasks, offering guidance through difficult times, or simply being present to listen and be patient. Through taking positive action, it is possible to positively reflect on the struggles of others and let them know that someone is there for them and will help them weather the storm.

If you want to build a truly successful business, start thinking about how you can positively impact the world. There's no better way to start than by practicing random acts of kindness.

RANDOM ACTS OF KINDNESS

Random acts of kindness can be as simple as holding the door open for someone, complimenting a stranger, or buying a cup of coffee for a coworker. These small gestures may seem insignificant but can greatly impact the people around you and your life.

For one thing, practicing random acts of kindness can help you build your network. When you go out of your way to help others, they will remember you and be more likely to help you. You never know when a small act of kindness could lead to a big opportunity.

However, more than that, practicing kindness will make you a happier person. Focusing on improving other people's lives, you'll find that your life feels more fulfilling. You'll feel like you're making a difference in the world, even if it's just one small act at a time.

As an entrepreneur, practicing kindness can help you build a business that truly makes a difference in the world. When you start your own company, getting caught up in your goals and ambitions is easy. However, if you want to create a business that people will love, focus on helping them. That starts with being kind.

As you journey from employee to entrepreneur, remember that small acts of kindness can have a big impact. Practice kindness every day. You'll soon find that it will become a natural part of who you are. You will also discover that it helps you build the successful, fulfilling life you've always dreamed of.

LIVING IN GRATITUDE

If there's one thing that can change your life in a heartbeat, it's gratitude. Living in gratitude is more than just being thankful for what you have; it's a way of life that requires you to cultivate a positive mindset that sees the good in everything you experience. When most entrepreneurs are asked what keeps them going through tough times, they often say an attitude of gratitude helps them push forward.

As you embark on your journey to entrepreneurship, it's important to realize that it won't always be easy. However, with a positive perspective, even difficult situations can turn into opportunities for growth and learning. Instead of focusing on what you don't have, try focusing on what you do have and all the amazing things around you.

One way to practice gratitude is to start a *Gratitude Journal*. Each day, take a few moments to write down 3 things you're thankful for. It could be as simple as the sunshine on your face or as big as closing a lucrative deal. The point is to reflect on the good in your life and take time to appreciate it. The more you practice this, the more you'll see the beauty in the world around you and the happier you'll become.

Another way to live in gratitude is to share it with others. When you make a habit of expressing your gratitude to those around you, you lift your spirits and those of the people you're interacting with.

It could be as simple as telling your team how much you appreciate their hard work or thanking a customer for their loyalty. Acts of kindness and gratitude have a ripple effect. You never know how far your positive energy can travel.

Living in gratitude means shifting your focus to the positive and choosing to see the beauty in every experience. It's not always easy, but the rewards are worth the effort.

As you embark on your journey from employee to entrepreneur and *Break Free from Your 9-to-5,* remember to practice gratitude and share the love with those around you. You'll be amazed at how much it can change your life and the lives of those around you.

In summary, enlightening others whose light may be dim is an important undertaking. It requires dedication and patience. Careful attention should be paid to creating an open and supportive atmosphere, recognizing individual feelings, and offering both conversation and practical support.

By following these steps, it is possible to offer much-needed light and hope to those struggling and needing help along the way.

A CLOSING NOTE FROM THE AUTHOR

Dear readers,

As I come to the end of this book, *Break Free from Your 9-to-5,* I want to take a moment to reflect on the journey that has brought us here.

When I decided to write this book, it came from a place of personal experience. As someone who has transitioned from employee to entrepreneur and broke free from my 9-to-5, I understood the challenges of this journey. I wanted to share my story and help others going through the same transition.

Throughout the book, I have shared stories and insights from my journey and lessons learned from other successful entrepreneurs. I have discussed topics like finding your passion, building a business plan, and transforming mentally and physically to show up as your best and authentic self to make a difference.

I also addressed the fears and doubts that come with starting your own business. It's important to understand that those feelings are normal; it's how you handle them that makes the difference. I encourage you to use those emotions to fuel your ambition and transformation.

One of the most valuable lessons I learned during my journey is the importance of building a support system.

Surrounding yourself with the right people can make all the difference in overcoming obstacles and reaching your goals, whether friends, family, or a mentor.

I also want to emphasize the importance of taking risks. As an employee, it's easy to fall into a comfort zone and avoid taking chances that may lead to failure. As an entrepreneur, I find it essential to be willing to take risks and try new things. Failures will happen. It's how you bounce back and learn from them that ultimately leads to success.

It is important to reflect on the journey you've taken. From the initial spark of inspiration to the realizable steps to launch a business, it is a unique path for each individual. You will find your methods, strategies, and processes to succeed as an entrepreneur.

Transitioning from employee to entrepreneur and breaking free from your 9-to-5 is a major life decision. Each aspect of the process requires dedication, hard work, and determination to achieve your dreams. Some key components include setting clear and attainable goals, developing a business plan, and finding a balance in your work and personal life. It's also important to keep an open mind and network with successful entrepreneurs.

As I end this book, I applaud your accomplishments! You have worked hard and showed great courage to pursue a dream. The journey to becoming an entrepreneur and breaking free from your 9-to-5 is long. You should be proud of how far you have come. No matter how successful or unsuccessful you may be, there will always be more to learn, new skills to gain, and new milestones to reach.

Make sure to never forget your passion and why you started on the journey in the first place. Although the process of becoming an entrepreneur may be challenging, it can be incredibly rewarding. If you remain at the helm of your destiny, choose to make the best of each day, and have passion and resilience, success will surely come.

Congratulations, and may your journey be prosperous!

Last, I want to remind you that building a successful business takes time and determination. It is not an overnight success; it is important to approach it with a long-term mind-set. Celebrate the small victories along the way and remain focused on the bigger picture.

In closing, I want to thank you for your interest in breaking free from your 9-to-5. I hope the lessons shared in this book have provided you with valuable insights and inspiration for your entrepreneurial journey.

No matter where you are on that journey, never stop learning, growing, and taking risks.

Wishing you all the best,
Phyllis Marlene Benstein

WHAT'S HOLDING YOU BACK FROM LIVING YOUR DREAM LIFE?

UNCOVER GAPS AND CREATE A PLAN FOR THE LIFE YOU DESERVE

Tired of feeling stuck, unmotivated, or unfulfilled in your career?

After reading this book, your next step is to take the Take Control of Your Life Assessment.

Discover the obstacles in your path and map out a clear action plan to create a life of *freedom and fulfillment.*

Take the first step toward your dream life now:
breakingfreefromyour9to5.com/assessment

EXHIBITS

EXHIBIT A

EASY-TO-USE CHECKLIST TO
BREAK FREE FROM YOUR 9-TO-5

Task	Notes	Check
Write a 1-pager about why you want to make this move.		
Embrace who you are at your core. Write your core values.		
Empower your evolution. Decide today to start on your corporate exit strategy. Write your exit date.		
Write your current list of life goals.		
Embark by doing things daily that will move you closer to your goal.		

Develop a daily, weekly, and monthly action plan.		
Determine your new business area: What type of business do you want to start, and what will you offer?		
Research the market, study the competition, and identify gaps you can fill with your business.		
Write your business plan.		
Get support from your family and friends.		
Analyze your finances. Determine your financial needs and resources.		
Establish a budget.		
Build your network. Form relationships with those who can help you.		
Choose a business name.		
Register your business and file paperwork with local, state, and federal tax authorities		
Purchase or rent any necessary equipment.		

Establish a work location.		
Set up a website.		
Set up your social media presence.		
Develop your marketing plan.		
Obtain necessary licenses and permits.		
Determine your pricing.		
Hire as necessary.		
Set up a bookkeeping system to track your income and expenditures for tax purposes.		
Set up a CRM.		
Launch your business.		
Evolve: Enjoy the journey; assess your current wardrobe and branding; adjust as needed.		
Enlighten: How will you make an impact on others and your communities?		
Write your plan for living, leading, and leaving your legacy.		

EXHIBIT B

RESOURCE LIST

Resource	Location	Check
Write your Business Plan	The local SBA provides *free* resources in most states, or we recommend you hire a business coach.	
Join your Local SBA	Google your area's Small Business Association; they provide free resources for you.	
Achieve Systems www.achievesystems-pro.com	Achieve Systems is a business-building membership program that provides you with everything you need from A to Z for $50 a month once you're a member—highly recommended.	
Connect & Collaborate www.connectandcol-laborate.co	Determine how to find leads for your business. We recommend growing location relationships through networking or opening your own group.	

Create your Marketing Plan	You can hire a coach or become an Achieve Systems member at www.achievesystemspro.com	
SCORE SCORE: Home page	SCORE is a non-profit organization that provides free mentorship and coaching to small business owners.	
Local Chambers of Commerce	Your local Chamber of Commerce can provide resources and connections to other business owners in your community	
Business.gov	A government website that provides information and resources for starting and growing a business.	
Entrepreneur.com	An online publication that offers articles, advice, and resources for small business owners and entrepreneurs.	
LinkedIn Learning	LinkedIn Learning offers online courses on business and entrepreneurship topics, from starting a business to marketing and finance.	
SBDCs	Small Business Development Centers offer free or low-cost training and resources for small business owners.	
NASBO nasbo.org	The National Association of Small Business Owners is a non-profit organization that offers resources and advocacy for small business owners.	

TED Talks	TED talks are a great source of education and inspiration. Many talks focus on innovation, leadership, and entrepreneurial success.	
Inc.com	This website is dedicated to helping entrepreneurs grow their businesses. It offers advice on everything from leadership and innovation to sales and marketing.	
Y Combinator ycombinator.com	This startup accelerator offers seed funding, mentorship, and resources for early-stage startups.	
AngelList AngelList: Build, Lead, Invest	A platform that connects startups with angel investors and a job board for startups looking to hire talent.	
TRE-UK https://streaklinks.com/ BQhArxdfn0YrwQAez QfUzrPI/https%3A%2 F%2Ftime2heal.treuk. com%2F%7Eaccess%- 2Fa50c185f%2F	Release your stress, recover, and discover a new you.	

EXHIBIT C

MALE/FEMALE SALARY COMPARISONS

In tech, specifically, *men were offered higher salaries than women for the same job title at the same company 59 percent of the time,* according to a 2021 survey from Hired. On average, women were offered salaries 2.5 percent less than the ones men were given for the same roles, according to a survey conducted on March 7, 2022 (survey source and info from Hired.com).

What is the pay rate difference between men and women?

March 15, 2022, is Equal Pay Day, which reflects how many extra days women had to work to make as much as men did in 2021. The gender wage gap persists; *women make 83 cents for every dollar a man makes.*

SOME THOUGHTS ABOUT WOMEN IN TECH AND SALARIES

The pay gap between men and women is a well-known issue in the world of technology. While women make up a small percentage of workers in the tech industry, studies have shown they earn significantly less compared to their male peers. This has unfortunately become an almost inescapable fact, often never realized until it's too late.

It's important to dive deeper into the reasons for this disparity. One common theory is that implicit bias leads to women being undervalued in the workplace. This could be from a lack of representation in leadership positions or the stereotype that women are not as technically skilled. It could also be combined factors of their age, attitude, behavior, and appearance. These implicit biases are difficult to pinpoint and address but remain a significant hurdle for women in the tech industry.

Another issue contributing to unequal pay in technology is women's lack of negotiation skills. It has been shown that women are less likely to negotiate for higher salaries when offered a job, as they may not want to come off as "aggressive" or may be afraid of losing the job offer altogether. This perpetuates the pay gap, as men are more likely to negotiate and push for higher salaries or benefits. This issue of gender imbalance in confidence cannot be stressed enough.

The lack of mentorship and promotions for women in tech is also a problem. If women are not given the same opportunities to advance in their careers, earning as much as their male counterparts is impossible. The technology industry needs more female role models, and men must become more proactive and vocal supporters of gender diversity and equity inclusion.

The journey from employee to entrepreneur requires hard work, dedication, and confidence, but it is not without its challenges. It's crucial for women to understand that they have the power to change the narrative and refuse to settle for unequal pay. It is vital to take risks and adopt the mindset that they are worth much more than what they have been offered or have been led to believe. Women need to learn to advocate for themselves and negotiate for their worth instead of depending on others to do that for them.

As we navigate the path to a more equal playing field for women in technology, it's essential to understand the issues that currently plague the industry. Gender imbalance and implicit biases are obstacles that can be overcome with small but meaningful changes in the mindset of all involved.

I also couldn't help but notice the stark difference in pay between men and women in ordinary jobs. This is something that has been talked about for decades, but it is still a prevalent issue in the workforce today.

According to the National Women's Law Center, women who work full-time and year-round still only earn about 82 cents for every dollar earned by men. This gap is even wider for women of color, with African American women earning 63 cents and Latina women earning 54 cents for every dollar earned by white, non-Hispanic men. This pay gap affects women's earnings and contributes to the gender wealth gap. Over time, this can lead to disparities in retirement savings, homeownership, and even access to health care.

Even more troubling is that this gap cannot be explained solely by differences in education or experience. Even after controlling for these factors, women still earn less than men.

This is why it's important for both employers and policymakers to take action to remedy this issue. Employers can start by conducting salary audits to ensure women and men are paid equitably for the same work. They can also commit to offering paid parental leave and flexible work arrangements, which are especially important for women who often bear the brunt of caregiving responsibilities.

Policymakers can also take action by strengthening equal pay laws and closing loopholes that allow employers to justify pay disparities. Providing affordable childcare and healthcare can also help lift the burden on women and allow them to fully participate in the workforce.

As an entrepreneur, it's essential to value and respect all employees' work, regardless of gender. We can create a more equitable and just society by acknowledging and addressing the pay gap between men and women.

Men have earned more than women since 1979, the first year with available data.

Median weekly earnings by gender

■ Men's weekly earnings   ■ Women's weekly earnings

Note: Dollar amounts are in 1982-84 CPI Adjusted Dollars. Data shows real earnings for full-time workers who are at least 16 years old.

Source: Bureau of Labor Statistics   INSIDER

Based on real weekly earnings data from the Bureau of Labor Statistics, the gap has narrowed over time.

ABOUT THE AUTHOR

Phyllis Marlene Benstein has a Bachelor of Science in Electrical Engineering (BSEE) and was previously employed as an engineer for 25 years. Phyllis' quantifiable result was saving millions in cost avoidance for her company and the DOD as a parts obsolescence management expert, where she was tasked with finding and developing solutions for converting obsolete parts into new sustainable designs.

Phyllis has created multiple, 7-figure businesses in the beauty, fashion, and networking industries. She was a founding leader of the fastest-growing global clean beauty and wellness company, with over $2 billion in revenue in 8.5 years. Phyllis has a history of leadership and training large organizations in and outside corporate. Phyllis is an international speaker and multiple best-selling author.

Professionals hire Phyllis to create additional revenue streams by transforming old designs and stories into new careers. Phyllis helps others efficiently monetize their businesses with multiple streams of income, creating their own economy.

As a sought-after, transformational expert through her knowledge of makeup and fashion and bolstered by her engineering, leadership, and networking background, Phyllis is a multi-faceted powerhouse. She leads professional workshops, keynotes, one-on-one coaching, and group presentations that are both enlightening and captivating. Additionally, Phyllis owns a networking brand called Connect & Collaborate, a division of Achieve Systems that gives entrepreneurs and small business owners the opportunity monthly to speak, sponsor, own, and/or attend chapter meetings in person and virtually worldwide.

Phyllis is an expert and raises awareness globally about the effects of toxins and what to avoid and provides awareness and education on mental health and wellness with holistic and natural products from Amare. Her engineering background has allowed her to see the world in a unique way. Phyllis always strives to build powerful relationships and help others find their powerful presence. She is proof that her processes and methods can help others go from geek to chic—and from ordinary to extraordinary. Phyllis creates a unique and winning formula for every client.

Phyllis is a master networker and connector. She is on a mission to serve others by helping them transform on the inside while having a rocking image on the outside in a way that fits their dream personality, lifestyle, and messaging that they need to radiate.

Phyllis Marlene Benstein would be honored to speak at your event. She is also available for one-on-one or group coaching for you and your team and organization. Visit her at https://www.linkedin.com/in/phyllismarlenebenstein to learn about her products and services and to join her communities.

Email: phyllis@phyllismarlene.com

Connect with her and let her know how she can best support you:

https://connectandcollaborate.co/network-with-me

Start your own networking chapter. Reach out for an interview: https://www.connectandcollaborate.co

Download your free Brain-Gut Correlation guide and learn about mental health optimization: https://www.phyllismarlene.com

Join the private Facebook community From Employee to Entrepreneur, Time to Transform https://www.facebook.com/groups/1357107207660614/

www.ingramcontent.com/pod-product-compliance
Lightning Source LLC
Chambersburg PA
CBHW031929190326
41519CB00007B/464